From New York to New Orleans

The 2002-03 Syracuse basketball team's journey to a championship

PRESENTED BY THE DAILY ORANGE

© May 2003
© July 2003, The Daily Orange Corporation
744 Ostrom Ave.
Syracuse, NY 13210

Telephone 315.443.2315

email: info@dailyorange.com
www.dailyorange.com

Library of Congress Cataloging-in-Publication Data

From New York To New Orleans:
The 2002-03 Syracuse basketball team's journey to a
national championship / presented by The Daily Orange
         p. cm.
   ISBN 0-9741487-0-9

1. Syracuse University — Basketball. 2. Syracuse Orange
(Basketball team). I. Daily Orange. II. Title.

GV885.43.S95F76 2003

796.323'63'0974766 — dc21

                                              2003010032

Designed by Kristin Ertel and Allyson Murphy

Contents

FOREWARD _____ I

SEASON RECORD _____ 3

PLAYER INFORMATION _____ 7

SEASON PLAY BY PLAY _____ 70

THE FINAL FOUR _____ 287

PHOTOGRAPHY CREDITS _____ 313

ACKNOWLEDGMENTS _____ 315

Foreward

After Carmelo Anthony's preseason Daily Orange photo shoot, he sheepishly smiled and asked us for a few proofs for his personal collection. We didn't know then how often he'd grace the pages of The Daily Orange — and later Sports Illustrated — or that the Syracuse men's basketball team would dominate the front page of newspapers nationwide by the 2002-03 season's end. By the time the Orangemen won the national championship, they had turned a puddle of student fans into a mass following and transformed critics' negative words into glowing praise. Indeed, the Orangemen's ride was a fairytale. And, in the following pages, The Daily Orange is proud to retell that story.

PETE IORIZZO, DARRYL SLATER & CHRIS CARLSON
THE DAILY ORANGE'S BASKETBALL BEAT WRITERS

2002-03 Season 30 WINS, 5 LOSSES

DATE	OPPONENT	LOCATION	SCORE
Nov. 5, 2002	Nike Elite*	Carrier Dome	W 93-74
Nov. 14	Memphis	Madison Square Garden	L 63-70
Nov. 19	Upstate N.Y. AAU*	Carrier Dome	W 110-88
Nov. 24	Valparaiso	Carrier Dome	W 81-66
Dec. 3	Colgate	Carrier Dome	W 98-68
Dec. 6	Cornell	Carrier Dome	W 85-62
Dec. 10	UNC-Greensboro	Carrier Dome	W 92-65
Dec. 14	Binghamton	Carrier Dome	W 94-58
Dec. 21	Georgia Tech	Carrier Dome	W 92-65
Dec. 28	Albany	Carrier Dome	W 109-79
Dec. 30	Canisius	Carrier Dome	W 87-69
Jan. 8, 2003	Seton Hall	Carrier Dome	W 70-66
Jan. 11	Boston College	Carrier Dome	W 82-74
Jan. 13	Missouri	Carrier Dome	W 76-69
Jan. 18	Pittsburgh	Petersen Events Center	L 60-73
Jan. 22	Seton Hall	Carrier Dome	W 83-65
Jan. 26	Miami	Miami Convocation Center	W 54-49
Jan. 29	Rutgers	Rutgers Athletic Center	L 65-68
Feb. 1	Pittsburgh	Carrier Dome	W 67-65
Feb. 3	Georgetown	Carrier Dome	W 88-80
Feb. 8	West Virginia	WVU Coliseum	W 94-80
Feb. 10	Connecticut	Hartford Civic Center	L 61-75
Feb. 15	Notre Dame	Carrier Dome	W 82-80
Feb. 18	St. John's	Carrier Dome	W 66-60
Feb. 23	Michigan State	Breslin Center	W 76-75
Feb. 26	West Virginia	Carrier Dome	W 89-51
March 1	Georgetown	MCI Center	W 93-84
March 4	Notre Dame	Joyce Center	W 92-88
March 9	Rutgers	Carrier Dome	W 83-74
March 13	Georgetown	Madison Square Garden	W 74-69
March 14	Connecticut	Madison Square Garden	L 67-80
March 21	Manhattan	Fleetcenter, Boston	W 76-65
March 23	Oklahoma State	Fleetcenter, Boston	W 68-56
March 28	Auburn	Pepsi Arena, Albany, N.Y.	W 79-78
March 30	Oklahoma	Pepsi Arena, Albany, N.Y.	W 63-47
April 5	Texas	Super Dome, New Orleans	W 95-84
April 7	Kansas	Super Dome, New Orleans	W 81-78

Big East Tournament (bracket spanning March 13–14)

NCAA Tournament (bracket spanning March 21–April 7)

* Exhibition

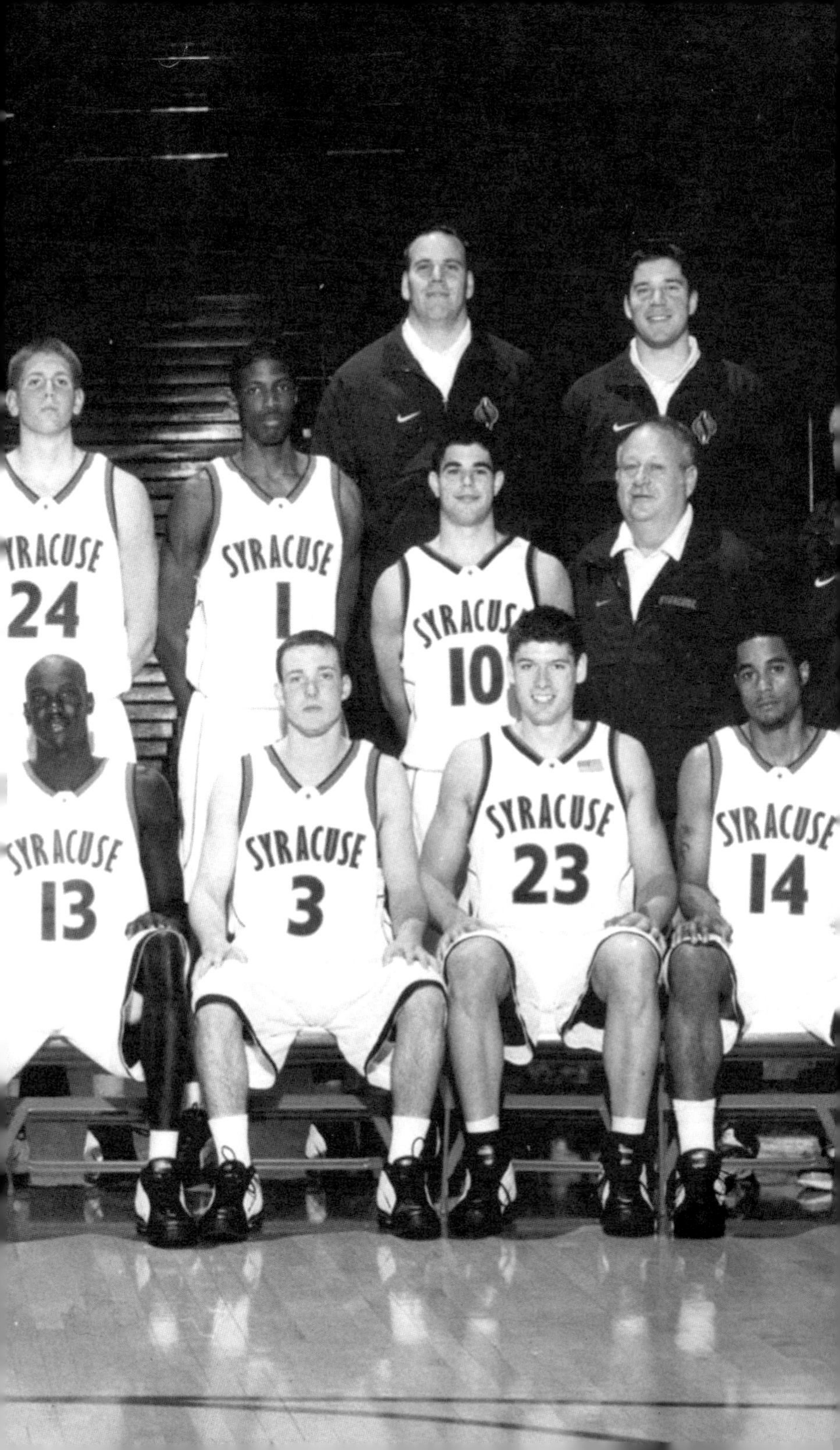
24
SYRACUSE
1
10
SYRACUSE
13
SYRACUSE
3
SYRACUSE
23
SYRACUSE
14

CARMELO
ANTHONY

#15 FORWARD

Height - 6-8 **Hometown** - Baltimore
Weight - 220 **High school** - Oak Hill Academy

2002 – 2003 STATISTICS

GP-GS	MIN	PTS	FG PCT
35 - 35	36.4	22.2	.453

3FG PCT	REB	AST	BLK
.337	10.0	2.2	30

Anthony adjusts to life at SU during first months

BY ELI SASLOW | 11.11.02

Eli Saslow will track Carmelo Anthony's Freshman year. This is the first story in a series.

The Nextel cell phone rings once before he reaches into his pants pocket and smothers it with his hand.

There are people around him. Lots of people. Still, curious about the call, he brings the phone up to his ear and hits the talk button.

"Hello."

"Yo, 'Melo, what's up?"

"Yo, what up?" he responds, a little louder, a little less apprehensive.

It's Troy Frazier, the man he talks to almost every day, the man who drove 300 miles to Syracuse from Baltimore just to watch a preseason scrimmage. Frazier's like an older brother, one of the people he spills his heart to.

"How you been?"

He's busy. Real busy. He's Carmelo Anthony, the No. 1-rated college basketball freshman in the nation, and in his two months at Syracuse, life hasn't slowed down very often. Nearly every day he spends three hours at practice with the Orangemen, an hour lifting weights to build his 6-foot-8, 220-pound body and another hour honing his jump shot.

He takes five classes — math, writing, psychology, education and African-American studies — and so far even his teachers admit he's only missed a couple. But just in case he falls behind, he spends several hours a week with a university tutor.

Even his down time isn't really his. When he walks across the Quad, three or four people come up to shake his hand or ask for an autograph. When he goes to Konrad's — as he does at 11:30 nearly every Thursday and Saturday night — he can't escape to a corner without a few girls following. When he goes to a party, he's bound to hear his name shouted on the microphone.

The attention's so overbearing that, in a reflective moment, he'll say, "I can't go anywhere and not be recognized. Nope, nowhere. Them days of just being me are over. From now on, I've got to be Carmelo Anthony, the superstar."

But he's not going to tell Frazier that. Not right now.

"I been good, man. Just chillin'."

"How's your game looking?"

"Feelin' good, bro. Feelin' real good."

Felt good since the first day he played pick-up basketball with the Syracuse team. When he walked into Manley Field House ready to scrimmage for the first time in late August, eight or nine teammates fixed their eyes intently on him.

They challenged him that day, senior Kueth Duany especially. They studied the 18-year-old who chose to take his scholarship to Syracuse instead of going straight from Oak Hill Academy — his high school in

Mouth of Wilson, Va. — to the National Basketball Association. All skeptics, his new teammates analyzed every step, looked to see if his moves measured up to his hype.

The Orangemen played for an hour. Afterward, Duany went straight to assistant coach Troy Weaver's office and said, "Coach, we're going to be good this year. You guys were right. He's even better than the press clippings."

When Anthony showed up to play pick-up the next day, his teammates called him "Franchise" and "The Chosen One." He's gone by those nicknames ever since.

"'Melo, man? You still there."

"Yeah, still here."

"How's the team, 'Melo. You all still kickin'?"

The team is, in fact, the best thing he's got going. When he came to Syracuse, he confided in his closest friends that he was worried he wouldn't fit in.

It took just one day on campus for him to find his crew. He drove to Syracuse with Frazier and his mother, Mary, on Aug. 24. He moved in with roommate Billy Edelin, met up with teammate Hakim Warrick and toured the campus. That night, the group went to Konrad's.

Since then, he's spent almost all his time with teammates Edelin, Warrick, Josh Pace and walk-on Andrew Kouwe. Sure, things hadn't been perfect at first. He told friends that he didn't get along with center Jeremy McNeil. And sometimes, when he was eating at Goldstein Student Center with the crew, he jumped on his cell phone to distance himself.

But before long, he felt at home. A few times while at Konrad's, the crew saved him, took him away from girls, stopped him from making a risky decision. He found friends — good ones. And the people who watched over him couldn't have been happier. Weaver, the assistant coach, told people, "That may be the most important thing for him. He fell into a great group of friends. That was huge for his transition."

"Yeah, of course things are still good, man. You know we tight."

"Yeah, just checkin' up. Life still treating you good?"

Better than ever. He's the hottest bachelor on campus: good-looking, always smiling and a probable lottery pick if he makes himself eligible for next year's NBA Draft. A few times, he's called friends from Konrad's.

"I'm dancing with five girls," he's said. "This is crazy. I love it."

A part of him always has loved the superstar role. He works hard during the day and goes out at night. He flirts with temptation but makes the right choices. Even Steve Smith, his coach at Oak Hill, knows him well enough to say, "I've never known him to have a girlfriend. But he always seems to have a few girls. Still, he walks that line well enough, makes the right decision enough to never get in trouble."

He'll call close friend Justin Gray — an Oak Hill teammate who's now a freshman basketball player at Wake Forest — and they'll talk about their problems. Gray will tell him, " 'Melo, I know you don't have a girlfriend. But that doesn't mean you can have a bunch of 'friends' either. Keep watching yourself."

He hears similar pleas from friend and Houston Rockets All-Star Steve Francis. He hears it from Frazier, too. He heeds the advice. He's exceedingly careful about who he spends time with and who he lets close to him.

"Yeah, everything's real good. And man, my body's getting cut. I'm looking real good."

" 'Melo, quit talking. You're still skinny."

He wants to talk about his chiseled upper body. He always does. It's the only thing he's cocky about.

Lifting weights an hour a day has paid off. It took him from scrawny to cut in two years. He loves to show off his chest, displaying the progress. He almost never wears a shirt at practice. Sometimes at parties, if he gets hot, he'll even take off his shirt and walk around barechested in a crowded room with music bumping in the background.

If he tells that to Frazier, he'll probably get lectured.

"All right, fine. But I'm telling you, I'm getting real big."

"So what you got next?"

Next? Everything's next. His season starts tonight at Madison Square Garden. He wants to be an All-American, the National Freshman of the Year. He wants to take the last shot in the closing seconds against Georgetown.

He will.

He wants to go out and have fun with the crew because, if he plays like he plans to, this could be his only year of college.

Next are expectations so big he tells his closest friends he doesn't want to think about them. Next is bulking up his chest so he can show it off some more. Next is finding a girlfriend or, more likely, another girl. Next is a year filled with promise and pressure, with elation and expectation.

"Next, I'm about to take a test. I'm in class and the teacher's passing one out."

"You've been in class this whole time?"

"Yeah, but it's a big lecture, so I don't think anyone really notices me." ∎

In his first game, Carmelo already acts like a star

BY ELI SASLOW | 12.6.02

Eli Saslow will cover Carmelo Anthony's freshman year. This is the second story in a series.

It took 20 minutes of basketball for freshman Carmelo Anthony to prove he could play like a superstar. And it took just a few minutes longer for him to show he could act like one, too.

After a dazzling 21-point first half against Memphis in Syracuse's season opener on Nov. 14, Anthony walked out for halftime and sat down with his back against the scorer's table. He stayed there with his legs stretched out onto the floor and admired the Madison Square Garden crowd while his teammates did layup drills.

"I was really relaxed," Anthony said afterward. "I felt in the zone. I didn't think I needed any extra few minutes of practice."

So far, he hasn't. Through three games — including a nationally-televised, 70-63 loss to Memphis in the Coaches vs. Cancer Classic — Anthony's averaging 27 points and 11 boards. While his defense has been suspect at times, Anthony leads the Big East in scoring and ranks second in the conference in rebounds.

Some close to Anthony say the early success has boosted his ego, but only slightly. What it's done most, though, is raise questions about Anthony's role with the Orangemen (2-1). Prior to the season, Anthony expected to be a main cog in a well-balanced Syracuse attack.

"Other guys can score," Anthony said then. "We've got a full team of good players. I want to be the go-to guy, but I don't have to be the guy all the time."

Through three games, Anthony's been Syracuse's only consistent scorer. He's scored at least 27 points in each game. Only one other Orangemen eclipsed 20 in a game (Kueth Duany had 21 on Tuesday against Colgate). Earlier this week, the lopsided offensive production seemed to have altered Anthony's team-oriented tune.

"Sometimes, I feel like I need to take this team on my back," Anthony said Tuesday. "Sometimes, I just feel like I need to take over."

Against Colgate, he ripped off 15 points in the first eight minutes,

helping Syracuse build a double-digit lead. He scored 11 points in less than five minutes in the second half against Valparaiso.

He's played 37 minutes a game, lugging around 25 pounds of muscle he didn't have last year.

"He's getting tired," head coach Jim Boeheim said. "He's in good shape but not good enough to play 37 minutes on offense and defense. He has to be our best rebounder and, obviously, our best scorer. We're asking a lot of him, there's no question."

Before the season began, some thought Syracuse wouldn't

ask for so much from the freshman. Anthony hoped to average a modest 16 or 17 points. Both Director of Athletics Jake Crouthamel and former Syracuse standout Pearl Washington said too much pressure on Anthony might hinder his development.

"He's got a cast of characters here that are capable," Crouthamel said before the season. "I'd be very surprised if he was going to be asked to put this team on his shoulders. I think problems or pressures would be more likely if he were asked to be the guy."

"He's a special player, but he's a freshman," Washington said. "Sometimes, you can't put all your stock in that. It might be a dangerous situation."

Syracuse seems to have little choice. With starters Duany (save his outburst earlier this week) and Craig Forth struggling and point guard Billy Edelin suspended, the Orangemen will have to hope Anthony doesn't wilt under the pressure.

But already, the long minutes and scoring burden seem to have affected parts of Anthony's game. A good free-throw shooter in high school, Anthony has made less than 60 percent from the line this year. Late in the game against Memphis, Anthony missed four straight free throws that could have kept Syracuse in the game. After the first miss, he walked away from the line in frustration. After the third, he gently pushed away Craig Forth's hand, which waited for a high five.

Against Colgate, Anthony missed 3 of 4 free-throw tries late in the first half. The next time he walked to the line, a few Syracuse fans screamed, "C'mon Shaq!"

Anthony's defense has suffered, too. Four times against Colgate, a player Anthony was responsible for nailed a three-pointer. Anthony admits his off-the-ball defense needs work. He's struggled to help fellow Orangemen who get beat down low.

"My main concern is that he's spending so much energy on offense that there's a diminished amount of energy on defense," Boeheim said after Syracuse beat Colgate. "He probably made 20 defensive mistakes in the first half."

After Syracuse beat Valparaiso on Nov. 24, one of Anthony's teammates had another concern. Late in the game when Valparaiso looked to foul, Anthony ended up shooting most of the free throws. Twice, Boeheim yelled to Anthony, urging him to pass the ball quickly and run more time off the clock. Anthony struggled to do so.

"He was pretty slow to pass," the teammate said. "He could have been looking at the stats a bit. But so far, that's not a big problem."

Two of Anthony's closest friends — Josh Pace and Hakim Warrick — insist the freshman does not worry about his stats and would not try to hold the ball to get fouled late in games.

"He's the exact same guy as he was before the season," Warrick said. "He's real relaxed, real cool. Nothing's changed except we got a new PlayStation. We play that more. That's the only thing that's different. (Anthony's) loving it right now."

"My confidence right now is extremely high," Anthony said. "If I need to score 30 points for us to win, then I'll do my best to score 'em." ■

No longer outspoken, Anthony ponders present

BY ELI SASLOW | I.29.03

Eli Saslow is covering Carmelo Anthony's freshman year. This is the third in a series.

He picks his words much more carefully now. Gone are the days when he'd smile at a reporter and say, "I'm leaving if I'm going to be a top-5 pick," or "It's always been my dream to play in the NBA."

Once capricious with his word choice, Carmelo Anthony — the SU basketball team's epicenter — now speaks about his future in vanilla phrases. His mind? "It's on the present." His thoughts? "On this season, not next."

It seems like a natural — perhaps even necessary — change for a college freshman that knows his words will be plastered all over the morning papers and regurgitated on newscasts. But those closest to Anthony — a likely lottery pick if he chooses to declare for next year's NBA Draft — say he's changed more than his verbiage. He's changed his thought process, too.

"He's gotten better about thinking about the present," said Troy Frazier, Anthony's close friend and mentor. "It's tempting for him to look ahead at all the possibilities. He used to fall into that a little bit. He's matured to the point where he only thinks about right now."

Good thing. Because if Anthony did peek to the future, he'd see that a circus surrounds him. Often, 10 or 15 scouts attend Syracuse games, mostly to watch Anthony's every stutter-step. Some people close to agents have started calling Anthony's friends and relatives, hoping to sway the superstar.

He's been featured in Sports Illustrated and during a halftime show on CBS. Big East players muse about his NBA future, certain he'll leave after one year. Frazier has decided he'll live with Anthony when he plays pro. Anthony's mother ponders where she will or won't live, because she wants to stay close to family in New York.

"If you start to think about all the stuff going on, it gets a little scary," said SU assistant coach Troy Weaver, who recruited Anthony. "He's not doing that. Really, he's done an amazing job keeping his mind at Syracuse and on the season."

Much of that is thanks to Weaver, Frazier and a few others, who've created a close-knit cocoon for Anthony where future plans aren't considered. Syracuse teammates say they don't talk to Anthony about the NBA, only the next college opponent. Weaver tells him to block out scouts who sit courtside, to forget they're even there.

Once or twice, Anthony's called Frazier — who attends almost every Syracuse game, home or away — to ask what scouts and agents might think about his basketball future.

"I don't care what they're thinking," Frazier told him. "And neither should you."

"When you've got all that commotion around you, it's important you don't see what's going on," Pearl Washington, a former SU star, said before the season. "(Anthony) will have to ignore it or block it out. That's the only way you'll get through the year."

So Anthony's essentially stopped answering the phone in his South Campus apartment. He won't pick up his cell phone unless he *knows* who's calling. His friends say he goes out less, choosing to spend more time with those he trusts.

"Everything else keeps moving and changing," said Steve Smith, his high school coach. "And he's still thinking and feeling the same."

He still loves the school, smiles big and generally revels in the Syracuse spotlight.

He still hates the weather and sometimes finds himself a little down when the campus is covered with snow and it's too cold to go out. His friends say he calls home more often when the weather's bad. And Frazier says, "the only time he thinks twice about his decision to go to college before the NBA is when it's a blizzard out."

"A lot of stuff might be going on around me," Anthony said, "but only two things have changed for me: The weather sucks, and we're playing the Big East schedule."

The latter has changed Anthony's basketball life significantly. For the first time since he can remember, he isn't finding all the answers on the court.

With defenses doubling or tripling him, he's averaging 16 points through five Big East games. That's less than teammates Hakim Warrick and Gerry McNamara in league play.

He hasn't led Syracuse in scoring in the last three games. In fact, he's only led the Orangemen once in their last seven. On Sunday at Miami, Anthony — who averages 21 points and nine rebounds — scored a mundane 12 points on 4-of-15 shooting.

"We keyed a lot of our defensive game plan toward stopping him," said Miami assistant coach Greg Gary. "Everyone's doing that now. He's impossible to guard. He can score inside and outside. The only way he won't score is if you keep him from touching the ball.

"Even if he doesn't touch it, he'll hurt you. He had 14 rebounds against us. If he doesn't, we probably win the game. He's one of the best players in this league. He should go (to the NBA after this year). He's one of those young guys you can tell is ready."

Other evaluators don't seem bothered by the dip in Anthony's scoring, either.

Said one NBA scout, speaking on a condition of anonymity: "You knew (the scoring lull) was going to happen. What's important is that he's kept his composure and distributed the ball. He's very good and very aggressive. Offensively, I don't see much about his game that needs to be picked apart. In basketball, when you're the center of attention, you have to adapt."

When you're the center of attention in life, you have to adapt, too. So, for now, Anthony speaks more carefully — if not thinks more carefully — and does his best to block out the circus.

"I'm not worrying about anything that's going on other than with this team," Anthony said. "I'll make a decision when the time comes." ∎

Sports world waits as Anthony weighs NBA choice

BY ELI SASLOW | 3.20.03

Eli Saslow is covering Carmelo Anthony's freshman season. This is the fourth story in a series.

Prankster. Goofball. You wanted that reputation, just so long as attention came with it.

One afternoon during your freshman year of high school, the entire student body sat quietly during an assembly and listened to a monotone voice. Not you. You stood up, hollered and tried to start the wave. You got a few laughs and detention. But the attention made you happy.

Now you're perched at a college basketball buffet, and attention's being shoveled at you any way you look. At 18, you drew the largest on-campus crowd in college basketball history. Ten days ago, 33,071 people packed the Carrier Dome and begged you to stay in college for another year.

Attention comes with responsibility now. It comes with big choices and bigger consequences. Everyone wants to choose for you, Carmelo Anthony, but the only choice that matters is your own.

You could return to college for a second year, invigorate a city, pose for the cover of Sports Illustrated's college basketball preview and be the superstar for a national title contender. Or you could turn pro, sign a multi-million dollar contract and buy a new house for your mom.

The sports world is waiting.

Scary, huh? You've never made these big decisions before. When you switched high schools, it was your mom's choice. When you waffled between Syracuse and the NBA as a senior, friends and family gave you the answer.

This time, they're telling you the choice is all yours. Attention's left you alone on an island. All you have to rely on are the survival skills you've learned the past five years.

When you turn on the television, you hear the media talk like you've already declared for the NBA Draft. You're one and done. A one-ride pony. As good as gone for next year.

Scouts and general managers expect you to leave because, well, who wouldn't? You're averaging 23 points and 10 boards as a freshman.

You're likely to be the No. 3 pick.

Even Troy Bell, the two-time Big East Player of the Year, thinks you'd be crazy not to go: "In terms of your draft status, you'll never be hotter. And for a kid without much money, those dollars have got to be tempting."

Million-dollar contracts were pure hyperbole on Murdle Avenue —

better known as Murder Ave. — where you grew up. A block from Baltimore's worst projects, you saw drugs, prostitution, crime and killing. Not money.

The one day you did have money, somebody robbed you. Fourteen years old and walking home from school, you got held up for $20. You stewed over losing that money for a week. Well, you can get it back now. You can fill a pool with twenties and show it off on "MTV Cribs." All you have to do is reach out and take it.

You're leaning toward staying in college.

It'll shock people. And that's one of the reasons you want to do it. Just a few weeks ago, you called up Syracuse assistant Troy Weaver and told him you were leaving for the NBA and you should have gone to Maryland. He had to call a couple of your friends before he figured out you were joking.

Keep people on edge. Shock them. Surprise them. That's how you work.

You've always done your own thing. Back in high school, you'd come out for warm-ups in a self-decorated T-shirt. Your teammates would wear the same colored shirt to look unified. You'd wear a white shirt with a slogan written on it. After a six-game, academic suspension, you came out in a T-shirt proclaiming, "I'M BACK."

The habit's stayed with you, though it's a bit milder now. For the Big East tournament, you wore a short-sleeved warm-up while the rest of the team wore long-sleeved shirts. You stood out, looked different. It brought you attention.

You're a people pleaser. That's the main reason you think you'll come back. You've always wanted — no, needed — to be liked. During a junior high baseball game, you missed your turn in the batting order because you were arguing. Your coach, Steve McClain, told you he was disappointed. So you spent the next three weeks showing up early and running wind sprints to appease him.

If you leave, a whole city will be disappointed. Fans have created a Web site, www.onemoreyear.com, on which they write messages to you. One poster wrote: "The bottom line is that we need you here. The fans, the basketball team, the University and the city need someone they can claim as their own, someone they can idolize."

A big request. But you want to give it to them because, if you do, they'll love you.

Billy Edelin, Josh Pace and Hakim Warrick — teammates who've become your closest friends — have told you that, if you come back, Syracuse could win a national championship. You don't want to let them down.

College life has won you over. For the first few weeks, you couldn't stop calling home. By Winter Break, you couldn't stand being more than a few blocks from your Syracuse friends. You were home in Baltimore for less than a week, and when your friends stopped by, they had to beg you to get off the phone with Warrick.

You're Big Man on Campus. Your team is winning. Awards are flowing in. Girls want a slice of you like you're everlasting pie. You're living every 18-year-old's dream. Hold off on your bling-bling, and you can do it all again next year.

One problem: Academics. First semester, you did great. You worked hard, went to class and finished with well above a 2.0. This time around, things aren't going quite so well. The travel and distractions of the Big East season have you hurting. Weaver called you into his office and told you: "If you go to the NBA, let it be your decision. Don't let being ineligible make the decision for you."

You took his words to heart. You're not in huge academic trouble, and it seems highly unlikely you could be deemed ineligible for next year. Still, you've rededicated yourself just in case.

A few days ago, your confidant Troy Frazier flew into Syracuse. He wanted a ride from the airport.

No, you told him. You had class.

"Damn, you really do want to stay another year," Frazier said. "Otherwise, you'd just be blowing this stuff off. This is a new Carmelo."

Just a matured one. And it took some tough lessons to get you here.

A bullet in the back took Tavares Graham, your older cousin, when you were a sophomore in high school. He'd lived with you, guided you, taken you under his wing like an older brother.

You called Eric Skeeters, a mentor of yours who'd coached Graham, and delivered the news.

You said: "Tavares got shot messing with the wrong people. I can't go like that."

Right away, your friends saw you grow up. Still a prankster, no longer a trouble maker. Calmer. Capable. Self-reliant.

So now they're telling you to make this decision on your own, to block out the thousands of voices whispering — if not chanting — in your ear and listen to your heart.

They've started to see you leaning.

A few weeks ago, BET came up to Syracuse to do a special on you. They wanted to feature a college athlete. They hoped to ride around in your car and hang out in your dorm room. Typically unexcited, you nearly slept through the interview. When Frazier asked you about it, you said:

"No big deal. If I'd slept through it, they could have just come up here and done it on me next year."

"So you're sure you're staying?"

Silence.

The sports world is waiting. ■

HAKIM
WARRICK

Height - 6-8 **Hometown** - Philadelphia
Weight - 205 **High school** - Friends Central

2002 – 2003 STATISTICS

GP-GS	MIN	PTS	FG PCT
35 - 35	32.7	14.8	.541

3FG PCT	REB	AST	BLK
.000	8.5	1.4	44

#1 FORWARD

Soft-spoken Warrick sneaks up on Big East with break-out year

BY ELI SASLOW | 1.28.03

Quiet. So quiet he's almost hard to talk to. That's what Hakim Warrick's mother says. She'll call her son at college and beg him to talk. Five minutes later, he's run out of words.

Shy. Shyest kid in the world, says his high school coach. He'd get a bad call, and the whole gym would start screaming. Except Warrick, who'd hand the ball to the referee and walk down court.

Low key. He won't leave his room unless you beg him to, says a Syracuse teammate. He'd rather spend a night at home with a few friends and his PlayStation than at a party with a few hundred admirers.

Quiet. Shy. Low key. Take your pick. But Warrick — a forward for the No. 24 Orangemen — dislikes them all.

"I'd go with sneaky," Warrick says. "I might be quiet, but I can come up on people. I can surprise you or shake things up just when you aren't expecting it."

Big East coaches and players are starting to take to Warrick's adjective. Through 15 games, the 6-foot-10 sophomore ranks in the conference's top 15 in points (16.8), rebounds (9.2), field-goal percentage (.575), steals (1.8) and blocks (1.3). Behind freshman Carmelo Anthony, he's the Orangemen's second-leading scorer and rebounder.

Typical of his entire basketball career, Warrick's progression to college stardom has occurred under the radar and without much fanfare. Sneaky almost.

"Right now, Warrick's probably the most improved player in the conference," says Greg Gary, an assistant coach at Miami. "He's not really known as a superstar, so a lot of people kind of fall asleep on him. You never think he's going to be the one to hurt you. But he always is."

He hurt Miami on Sunday with a game-high 18 points, including a fatal put-back dunk with five minutes left that gave Syracuse the lead for good. He buried Seton Hall on Wednesday with a team-high 22 points and 10 boards. He dropped 20 on Missouri and 24 on Boston College earlier this month.

"He's played his best in big games," says teammate and roommate Josh Pace. "He's stepped up pretty much every time this year. He's turning into a giant killer."

Funny. Last year, Warrick got killed by the giants.

Long and athletic, Warrick started his college career with swooping dunks against the likes of Binghamton, Colgate and Cornell. He'd use his reach to grab rebounds over shorter players and use his hops to jump over opponents for improbable jams.

In just the seventh game of his college career, he scored 22 points and grabbed 11 boards in 22 minutes against Cornell. He dunked seven times, often bringing the Carrier Dome crowd to its feet.

"We knew right away he was super-athletic," teammate Kueth Duany said. "He could do things that nobody else on the team could do. You could tell he had the potential to be unbelievable."

Intolerable. That's how SU head coach Jim Boeheim described Warrick's play in SU's Big East opener last year against Rutgers. Then-Scarlet Knights forward Rashod Kent had 100 pounds on Warrick — and he used all of it. In the first half, Kent bumped and bruised Warrick under the basket. The abuse lasted three minutes. Then Boeheim sat Warrick for the rest of the game.

With the onset of the Big East season, Warrick lost minutes and, he thought, his coach's respect. In practices, he felt picked on more than any other teammate. In games, he never knew if he'd play 15 minutes or not at all.

At season's end, he averaged six points and five rebounds in 17 minutes.

"If you look at his numbers, they were pretty good," says Queen Warrick, Hakim's mother. "But he was miserable for a little while there. He thought Coach Boeheim was picking on him. He thought he was in the doghouse.

"For a while, he mentioned transferring. But that was never really serious. He always knew he'd do what he always does: be quiet and stick it out."

Or, in Warrick's words: be sneaky and stick it to 'em. That's the path he'd taken when recruiters showed little or no interest in Warrick when he was a lanky junior at Friends Central outside Philadelphia.

Despite averaging 15 points and 14 rebounds, Warrick remained relatively unknown in recruiting circles. That is until a last-minute fluke connection landed him at the Nike Camp, a recruiting extravaganza packed with prep stars and high-profile coaches. There, Warrick flashed enough of his jump-out-of-the-gym athleticism to garner interest from Syracuse and Villanova.

When another potential Syracuse recruit, Julius Hodge, decided on North Carolina State, the Orangemen offered their fifth and final scholarship to Warrick. Having fallen in love with the school on a recruiting visit, Warrick accepted.

"He came out of nowhere to get those offers to two top schools," says Keino Terrell, Warrick's high school coach. "He got that opportunity at the Nike Camp and just decided, 'These guys might not know me, but they will soon.' "

"I just kind of came up on people," Warrick said. "All of a sudden people recognized I could play. It's kind of similar to what's happening this year. I've just kind of snuck up onto the scene."

And true to form, he's done so quietly. He's often hid behind his best friend Anthony, the No. 1-ranked freshman in the country and a likely lottery pick if he chooses to declare for next year's NBA Draft.

Opponents key on stopping Anthony; Warrick sneaks in for easy baskets. Anthony gets articles in Sports Illustrated and halftime features on CBS; Warrick gets to sit by his locker unbothered. Anthony's boisterous; Warrick's shy.

"It's definitely helping Warrick that Anthony soaks up all the attention," says Gary, the Miami assistant. "We spent all week watching film of Anthony, breaking him down. It makes you kind of forget about the other guys."

Which is fine by Warrick. It'll give him the chance to surprise opponents and keep using his favorite adjective: sneaky. ∎

GERRY
M^CNAMARA

Height - 6-2   Hometown - Scranton, Pa.
Weight - 172   High school - Bishop Hannan

2002 - 2003
STATISTICS

#3 - GUARD

GP-GS	MIN	PTS	FG PCT
35 - 35	35.3	13.3	.401
3FG PCT	REB	AST	BLK
.357	2.3	4.4	2

With every basket, McNamara lifts an entire community

BY CHICO HARLAN | 2.20.03

SCRANTON, Pa. — Cheers, to Gerry McNamara, from the Guinness line at Cosgrove's Clubhouse & Tavern, where never before could one 19-year-old Irish boy claim so many unacquainted cousins.

Cheers from the Carrier Dome upper deck and its 52 busloads of adoring Scrantonians — 2,000 in all — who marched two hours north to flute their support, in a fan club called "McNamara's Band," for a freshman point guard scoring 14.3 points per game.

Cheers from the employees at Stirna's restaurant, just seven blocks from McNamara's childhood home in North Scranton. Raise a glass, because suddenly, with one heroic 3-point shot and one euphoric riot of people fixed before a 22-inch television, opening four hours early for a 1 p.m. Syracuse basketball game didn't seem so silly anymore.

Here's to Gerry McNamara, the toast of Scranton, Pa. The hero, the role model, the kid with a jump shot who's made a steely town of 75,640 feel cozier than a Holy Rosary church meeting. His game-winning 3-pointer against Notre Dame on Saturday, the one that gave Scranton the ending it hoped for? That's all dandy, but any fairy-tale ending requires a fairy-tale story to begin with.

This one begins with a town and its pride for a teenager, a pride so strong that the simple mention of the teenager's name can turn two strangers in Scranton — young or old, it doesn't matter — into playground pals or golfing partners or drinking buddies. So by now, because of McNamara, it's safe to say Scranton's pretty much run out of strangers.

"He helps people here make a connection," Tommy Bell, an assistant coach of McNamara's in high school, said at Cosgrove's the night before the Notre Dame game. "People see Gerry on ESPN or at the Carrier Dome, and they know: This is Gerry McNamara. He lives on West Market Street. He has a little white-paneled house. His parents work at the post office."

At once, McNamara's an everyman and a talisman. Like much of Scranton's populace, McNamara sprouts from proud Irish roots and a tight knitting of family and community. But in a town where generations live and die in the same house, hire and retire in the same jobs, McNamara's success spurs the following.

"In this area, nobody's ever gotten more attention," said Billy Clark.

Clark's responsible for a small part of it, because for most SU home games, his company, Cookies Travelers, charters several buses from

Scranton to Syracuse. On Saturday morning, Clark's line of eight buses greeted a parking lot of Scrantonians at 8:30 and fumed north on Interstate 81, 450 people aboard.

Come game time, roughly one of every 37 Scranton residents — including 200 of the town's 220 police officers — filed into the Carrier Dome. The fans displayed clementine-colored "McNamara's Band" signs, distributed by the local Scranton paper, and wore No. 3 jerseys and T-shirts, some store-bought and many homemade.

Scranton lacks any notable professional or college teams, so many in northeastern Pennsylvania root for Notre Dame. That partially explains why Saturday's game with the Irish drew the largest crowd yet from Scranton. But since McNamara signed on at Syracuse, the Irish cognoscenti signed off their allegiances to Notre Dame — or, if nothing else, leased them away for four years.

"This is the first time in my life I'm rooting against the Irish," Scranton resident Jim O'Shea said on the bus ride. "I have my Irish underwear on, but nobody can see it."

Everything's about Syracuse now, because, as one student said after a Bishop Hannan high school basketball game Friday night, "Gerry's basically taken Scranton over." McNamara played four years at Hannan, drawing considerable attention and press while earning the school a state championship his senior year.

"But now," said Hannan principal James Marcks, "it's grown from a Bishop Hannan thing into a Scranton thing."

By eighth grade, McNamara eclipsed the popularity of the town mayor, who happened to be McNamara's uncle. Come high school, Jimmy Connors wasn't "the mayor of Scranton." Rather, in a turn of good politicking that kept him in office for three terms, his identity became "Gerry McNamara's uncle."

"That's when I knew we had a phenomenon here," Connors said.

So if that's a phenomenon, what's this? Maybe it's best stated, as one patron suggested at Cosgrove's, like this: Gerry McNamara is more loved by Scranton than any other person is loved in any other place.

Consider that when two student reporters from this newspaper drove to Scranton for an article on McNamara, WYOU-TV, the local CBS affiliate, interviewed the SU students for its lead on the 11:00 news, two stories before the first mention of Iraq.

"Around here," an employee at a local sporting goods store said, "McNamara gets more press than George Bush."

He also gets more adulation, as 10-year-old Scrantonian Austin Trubia affirmed on the bus ride to Syracuse last Saturday. For an elementary school project, students picked one person, a leader or role model, about whom to research and write. Trubia opted for Los Angeles Lakers star Shaquille O'Neal, who seemed like a worthwhile selection until the

fifth-grader arrived in school to find that every other boy in the class had picked McNamara.

Even in high schools across Scranton, the veneration's no less. Before a Bishop Hannan basketball game earlier this season, an opponent on rival Riverside walked through the pregame shootaround wearing a replica McNamara Syracuse jersey. As one Bishop Hannan teacher put it, McNamara, at once both revered and celebrated, plays the role of Scranton's Santa Claus.

Sideburns substituted for shag, of course.

"When Scranton has somebody who makes it big — and that's not too often — the people here love it," said Phil Yacuboski, a news anchor at WYOU. "He's the hometown hero, and he's only (19)."

"We just can't keep up with how big it's gotten," said McNamara's mother, Joyce.

Chiz McNamara has become pretty big in his own right, which is to say, everybody in town knows he's Gerry's father. Nowhere was that more evident than at Scranton High's 3,000-seat gym, where Chiz stood against a wall by the baseline to watch a Gerry-less Bishop Hannan team play in the district playoffs Friday, 12 hours before he'd travel to Syracuse and watch his son.

After Hannan dropped the game in overtime — "Boy, sure coulda used Gerry tonight," one observer remarked as Hannan junior Matt Blume missed 2 of 3 late free throws — Chiz bottlenecked the gym entrance while exchanging pleasantries with well-wisher after well-wisher.

Thirty-seven handshakes, four kisses and countless, *You goin' up tomorrow?*'s later, Chiz and his wife left an empty gym.

"It's amazing," said Chiz, whose real name, Gerry, has been long since overwritten by his nickname. "Just shaking hands with all these people, and a lot of them have been following Gerry since he was in seventh or eighth grade."

During childhood, McNamara honed his game on an elevated stage of pavement — barely large enough for a pick-up truck — in his backyard. A slanted Action Force basketball hoop manicured McNamara's jump shot, although Blume, the Hannan junior and a family friend, remembers that McNamara would sometimes fall off the ledge while shooting long-range jumpers.

Since moving to larger stages, McNamara's practice has been

well-served. En route to being named 2002 Player of the Year in Pennsylvania, the 6-foot-2 guard led Bishop Hannan to a state championship. But listen to the stories that spill through Cosgrove's Tavern and you'll see that another McNamara moment trumped even the state title.

A game earlier, in the state semifinal against defending-champ Trinity, McNamara wrote Scranton's best-ever barbershop tall tale by pouring in 55 points — 41 in the first half. That two-quarter stretch included nine 3-pointers.

"Never seen anything like it," Bell, the Hannan assistant, remembered. "He was unconscious. People were literally running out of the gym at halftime with their cell phones. Like, 'Hey, you wouldn't believe what I'm seeing right now.'"

As Bell, just one sunrise from a 130-mile drive to Syracuse, relayed the story at Cosgrove's last Friday night, the playoff loss that transpired several hours earlier seemed long forgotten.

Here, McNamara is the panacea. The inspiration. The impetus to raise 75,000 glasses. An iconography of Rocknes and Horsemen clutter every wall in every pub, but come game day, McNamara is the icon who's responsible for filling every barstool in town.

"He truly is an icon," said a Bishop Hannan janitor named Tommy. "I've never seen one person change everything so quickly. People see what he can do, and now there's hope for everyone."

Make no mistake, Scranton doesn't need McNamara. For the last century, it's done just fine with a status quo, so what's another generation of the same? There's a certain charm to a place where a solicitation for directions prompts a 10-minute conversation. Or to a place where restaurant owners will introduce themselves on the rare occasion that an out-of-towner walks in. Or to a place where high school sports keep a safe perspective but also attract enough interest to make them worthwhile.

"The people of Scranton feel like they're part of it," NFL Hall of Famer Mike Munchak said. "They watched you grow up, and they don't forget about you when you leave. That just doesn't happen anywhere else."

Until McNamara, Munchak remained Scranton's most celebrated athlete. Munchak graduated from Scranton Central in 1978. He advanced to Penn State and later to the NFL's Houston Oilers, where he was a perennial Pro Bowler on the offensive line.

Yet even Munchak admits that he never surpassed the status of "mini celebrity." McNamara, as 10-year-old Trubia points out, "is bigger than a movie star."

He did nothing to detract from that reputation Saturday.

Movie star grew into Oscar winner when McNamara flashed open on the baseline with 22 seconds left and Syracuse down, 80-79, to the Irish. Shoulders squared and feet pegged just behind the 3-point arc, McNamara accepted the pass from guard Billy Edelin and converted on what he'd later call his biggest shot of the year.

"He wasn't going to let 2,000 people from Scranton down today," Syracuse head coach Jim Boeheim said after the 82-80 SU win.

An hour after the shot, McNamara, still in uniform, strode from the locker room back onto the Carrier Dome court, where he celebrated with roughly 30 relatives and friends while signing autographs for a short line of children.

By nightfall, though, nearly every Scrantonian in the building would return home, back to their families and friends, their jobs and their churches, their pubs and their restaurants. And McNamara, with nothing more than a jump shot, would continue to make all of those things pretty darn enjoyable. ■

KUETH DUANY

Height - 6-6 Hometown - Bloomington, Ind.
Weight - 185 High school - Bloomington North

#13 - GUARD

2002 - 2003 STATISTICS

GP-GS	MIN	PTS	FG PCT
35 - 35	27.0	11	.439
3FG PCT	**REB**	**AST**	**BLK**
.350	3.7	2	17

Finally, Boeheim's screams turn to praise for senior Duany

BY DARRYL SLATER | 2.27.03

Kueth Duany's ears can perk to it by now, that nasally scream from the sideline.

Every game, it seems, Duany hears Syracuse men's basketball head coach Jim Boeheim yell his name: "Kuuueth!" It's an unmistakable shriek, usually accompanied by Boeheim cupping his hands around his mouth, often prompted by a Duany mistake.

Last night, though, in the No. 15 Orangemen's 89-51 win over West Virginia, Boeheim yelled Duany's name once, as the fifth-year senior scored 18 points, his most since Jan. 8, when he dropped 20 on Seton Hall.

But Duany swears he heard two Boeheim screeches.

"I think it was twice for defensive purposes," Duany said. "I don't think he'd feel complete if he didn't yell at me."

Said Boeheim: "Defensively, Kueth had his best game."

Indeed, Duany shut down WVU's Drew Schifino, holding the guard to 4-of-18 shooting for 10 points.

"That was my pinpoint," Duany said, "to guard Schifino and slow him down, basically be in his face every time he got the ball."

But Duany, whose SU career is marked more by scrappy defense than flashy offense, found his shot early, scoring the Orangemen's first five points, en route to a team-high 13 by halftime. As SU's main scoring options struggled — forward Carmelo Anthony scored his first point 8:07 into the first half — Duany kept the Orangemen close before they blew the game open.

"He didn't think about (shooting)," SU guard Billy Edelin said. "Sometimes, when he misses his first couple early, he starts getting upset."

Duany, who's fourth on SU with 12.3 points per game, found a different explanation for his quick start.

"They left me open," he said with a smile. "That's what happened."

On a Syracuse team rife with scoring threats (see: Anthony, guard Gerry McNamara and forward Hakim Warrick), opponents often forget Duany. Though he's six points shy of 1,000 for his career, he admitted, "I've never been known as a scorer."

Still, Duany takes his offensive game seriously. He's the first Orangeman on the floor at every practice, honing his jump shot with assistant coach Troy Weaver. He's bristled at the notion that he needs extra help with his shot and has said, "I've always been able to shoot."

When asked last night whether he feels opponents don't respect his offensive game enough, Duany shrugged and said, "Maybe. But I've

killed a lot of teams, so they can continue to disrespect me."

Duany's teammates revere him, if for nothing else than the constant verbal abuse he takes from Boeheim. The coach reserved a V.I.P. suite in his doghouse for Duany since the day the 6-foot-6 guard arrived on campus, though Duany said he's not sure why.

"Of course, nobody likes to get screamed and hollered at," Duany said. "But I've accepted it. That's the way it's always been."

Said Warrick: "I've learned a lot from Kueth. Coach gets on me a lot, but I know it's not half as bad as him."

Boeheim's shrieks toughened Duany for late-game situations, said SU assistant coach Mike Hopkins, who works with the Orangemen's guards.

"(Duany's) one of those guys," Hopkins said, "who, if things aren't going well, he'll work harder."

Said McNamara: "He puts up with a lot from Coach, but he responds to it."

So as Duany stripped the tape off his ankles last night, he paused for a moment, perhaps thinking how quiet the court seemed. No shrieks or screams. Barely a holler. Just a lot of open space.

"I got some real easy looks tonight," Duany said, "and I knocked them down."

Easy? Well, on his ears. At least for a night. ∎

CRAIG
FORTH

Height - 7-0 **Hometown -** East Greenbush, N.Y.
Weight - 265 **High school -** Columbia

 # 51 – CENTER

2002 – 2003
STATISTICS

GP-GS	MIN	PTS	FG PCT
35 - 35	17.7	3.8	.487

3FG PCT	REB	AST	BLK
.000	3.3	0.9	41

Though hard on himself, Forth always eager to lift others

BY DARRYL SLATER | 11.10.02

It was always a battle. The over-ambitious 12-year-old trying to get something — a smile, a nod even — out of his 3-year-old brother.

"Jeremy, point to blue," Craig would say.

Jeremy's head would swivel, his eyes darting around the kitchen in search of a distraction. His arms would flail, as he tried to speak and fight the autism that had turned his mind into a prison.

"No, Jeremy," Craig begged. "Over here! Blue!"

The daily exercises would go on like this for hours. But Craig — ever the perfectionist — never gave up.

Syracuse men's basketball player Craig Forth can never do enough for himself.

Though the 7-foot Forth started every game at center and averaged 4.9 points last season as a freshman, he picked apart his play after every game.

After all, for so long, he's let other people lean on his strength. He'd give and give. He'd give his time — to working on his game, to his brother, to a friendship with a disabled girl in high school, but never to himself.

And when he couldn't give anymore, he'd tear himself apart.

But, as always, he's expecting more this year. He's honed his footwork. He's bulked up.

"I've always been in a rush to please everybody," he says. "Now, this year, I'm in a rush to please myself, play the way I want to play. I want to be my own person, my own player."

For 15 minutes, Forth stands in the Carrier Dome's muggy locker room, hanging his head. He's done this far too often in SU's disappointing 2001-02 season.

Answering every postgame question, he blames himself. No toughness on the boards, too many stupid fouls, he says.

He's 18 years old and SU's lone regular freshman starter. But it's never enough, because when he goes home he'll hear the praise — *We're so proud of you, Craig. You're doing such a great job.* And since he's always been so over-ambitious — with volunteer work, with basketball, with Jeremy — he's rushed to please everyone else first.

"(Hearing praise) always makes me want to do so much more,"

Forth says. "When I think that I'm not doing a great job is when it just kills me."

So Forth worked himself to the bone last year. He was so busy that he barely slept and ate. By season's start, he'd lost 15 pounds, starting his first SU game at 255 pounds, his lowest playing weight since his freshman year at Columbia High in the Albany suburb of East Greenbush.

In SU's 23-13 season, in which the Orangemen lost eight of their last 12 regular-season games, Forth averaged 4.5 rebounds and blocked a team-leading 65 shots.

Still, Forth averaged three fouls and fouled out four times.

"Starting every game was a great experience for me last year," he says. "But was I at the right weight to do it? Was I at the right mental capacity to do it? I don't think so."

The suddenly frail Forth played standing straight up — rather than staying low as SU assistant coach Bernie Fine preached — and spent plenty of time picking himself up off the floor.

He admits now that, at first, he couldn't keep up with college competition.

"Last year was embarrassing," he says. "I watch games where I fell down like 15 or 20 times each game."

After three hours of drills, Carmelo Anthony was getting bored.

Anthony, SU's prized freshman, started playfully shoving sophomore Josh Pace during wind sprints in a preseason practice. Forth stepped back and rolled his eyes.

"Come on guys," Forth said. "This is the last sprint, let's go."

Forth's been an on-court director since last year, when he'd loudly correct fellow center Jeremy McNeil whenever he got out of position.

This year, teammates and coaches are expecting Forth to continue that role and assert himself more physically down low.

"Craig is much bigger this year, he's much stronger and he's much improved," SU head coach Jim Boeheim says. "We're going to expect some things from him."

Indeed, Forth says he packed on 25 pounds during the summer.

"I think I have a six-pack," he says. "But I'm not sure."

"The No. 1 thing for Craig," says Jim Obermeyer, Forth's high school coach, "was just to get bigger and stronger, and I think he's done that. It doesn't take him long to figure things out. I remember when he was in eighth grade, the knock on him was that he didn't get from one end of the court to the other very well. By 10th grade, he was pretty good at changing ends."

Forth spent part of his summer at the Pete Newell Big Man Camp in Hawaii, working with NBA coaches and players. He brushed up on his shoddy footwork, which last year made him look a step too slow.

"He knows he was challenged last year," SU guard Kueth Duany says. "But he's done a lot of growing up since then."

At Columbia High, Jaime Adams is always the quietest cheerleader.

She sits in her wheelchair on the sidelines, her body ravaged by Rett Syndrome. She can't walk, she can't speak. Her dad, Burke, waves her pom-poms for her because she can't move her hands.

When she was 4, Jaime was diagnosed with Rett, a neurological disorder that hampers communication and motor skills. By age 8, she weighed just 20 pounds. For seven years, Burke couldn't even look at his blonde-haired, blue-eyed baby girl without crying.

Jaime just turned 18, and this year will be her eighth as a Columbia

cheerleader. Her favorite player is the school's all-time leading scorer — Craig Forth.

"She can't talk, but you can tell by her eyes," Burke says. "She loves that Craig. He's always been her helper."

Before Columbia's Senior Night game in 2001, the Blue Devil seniors gave bouquets of flowers to senior cheerleaders. Forth gave his to Jaime.

"There wasn't a dry eye in the house," Obermeyer says.

When Forth broke the school scoring record, he ran over to Jaime, kissed her on the cheek and gave her the ball. It still sits in her room.

"When Craig comes over to our house to visit," Burke says, "Jaime will be laying on the floor, because she can't sit up, and I'll say, 'Your buddy Craig is coming.' She'll roll her eyes back, because he used to sneak up from behind her. She'll always remember when he does that. She'll just get a big smile on her face."

In high school, Forth worked with Burke and Jaime in basketball, softball and soccer leagues for disabled kids.

Forth, of course, always pushed Jaime around the bases.

"She loves those bumpy rides around the bases," Burke says. "She laughs so hard when she goes around the bases. Craig's leaning over, saying, 'Jamie, how was that?' And she looks back at him like, 'Keep going.' "

Forth's been helping disabled kids as a peer mentor since third grade. But Jeremy and Jaime's influence on his life further fueled his passion to become a special education teacher.

Forth remembers how his mother, Maggie, used to tell Jeremy's kindergarten teachers what worked best to help Jeremy open up. The teachers, wouldn't listen.

"If he couldn't get the things that my mom wanted for him," says Forth, an inclusive education major who's now student-teaching at Salem Hyde Elementary School, "I'm going to be the teacher that

gives other kids like Jeremy what his parents want."

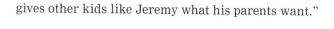

Forth lives for the phone calls from his younger brother.

They come as a relief when he's sitting in his South Campus apartment, stressed from a full day of classes, exhausted from a torturous practice.

He'll pick up the receiver and hear that soft voice, still struggling to squeeze out a word.

"Jeremy," Craig asks, "what'd you do in school today?"

"Me ... and the teacher ... and Miss Wilcox ... and everybody ... went over ... to the apple farm ... and picked apples."

It's progress. And it's a reminder to Forth that the time he spent working with his autistic brother made a difference.

"Talking like that over the phone is huge," Forth says. "Before it would be like, 'Jeremy, you have to look at me,' or else he wouldn't talk to you. I'm so proud of him."

On the outside of Forth's right ankle, above the super-sized Birkenstock sandals he's wearing, is a Chinese symbol tattoo.

"It means strength," Forth says.

In a sense, that's never been a problem for him. ∎

BILLY
EDELIN

Height - 6-4 Hometown - Silver Spring, Md.
Weight - 195 High school - Oak Hill Academy

2002 – 2003 STATISTICS

GP-GS	MIN	PTS	FG PCT
23 - 0	23.2	9	.548
3FG PCT	**REB**	**AST**	**BLK**
.000	3.4	2.5	2

#14 – GUARD

Edelin's Maryland friends see 'Same Old Billy' on the court

BY DARRYL SLATER | 2.4.03

Frank Bell got the call one Sunday night.

It was Billy Edelin, his little brother's friend since second grade.

Edelin urged Bell and his little brother, Erick, to make the six-hour drive from Silver Spring, Md., for Syracuse's Feb. 3 game against Georgetown. After all, since the day Edelin committed to Syracuse, he's been trash-talking Frank, a Hoyas fan.

So Frank donned a Georgetown hat and jersey, Erick slipped into similar Syracuse attire and the brothers settled into their Carrier Dome

seats to root on their boyhood friend.

Edelin didn't disappoint. In the Orangemen's 88-80 win, he scored 10 points, dished three assists and had just two turnovers in 25 minutes.

"Same old Billy," Frank said, shaking his head as he sat on a chair in the SU locker room.

"I just got minutes," Edelin said as his friends looked on. "Coach got me in there earlier, and things started off well. Sometimes, when you get less minutes, you're more likely to force something. When you get minutes, you can let things come to you."

Indeed, when Edelin played 28 minutes against Seton Hall, he scored 11 points. In 33 minutes at Rutgers, he had eight points and four assists. Edelin went scoreless in 14 minutes at Miami, and in his debut at Pitt on Jan. 18, he had two points in seven minutes.

If more playing time didn't get Edelin hyped, familiar company certainly helped. During his time at DeMatha High, Edelin played against Georgetown's Drew Hall, Tony Bethel and Mike Sweetney.

Hall called Edelin at SU's team hotel the night before the game to wish him luck.

"We've been talking about this game a little bit since the beginning of the season," said SU forward Carmelo Anthony, Edelin's roommate.

"Before this game, (Edelin) was extra hyped," SU forward Hakim Warrick said. "He was saying, 'We can't lose this game.' "

Edelin entered Feb. 3's game 4:28 into the first half. Within 15 seconds, he nailed a floater, his favorite shot.

"I felt good after that," he said.

With 3:34 left in the first half, Edelin dished a no-look pass to SU center Craig Forth, who converted a short jump shot to put the Orangemen up, 40-34. Edelin scored four of SU's last six first-half points. Eight minutes into the second half, he found Jeremy McNeil for a dunk that gave SU a 59-56 lead.

Edelin sprinted down the court, pumping his fist and yelling, "What!"

"I like to get the team fired up," Edelin said. "Sometimes we'll be leading by two or three points, and we look like we're dead. So I try to get everybody hyped."

"He was just on-point with us," Syracuse forward Kueth Duany said. "He had a lot of energy, and that's what we needed. (The biggest things he had to get used to were) knowing where guys like the ball and knowing where other guys are gonna be on the court. Throwing a new guy out there, it takes time."

Playing point guard against the Hoyas, Edelin looked the most comfortable he has all season. He hesitated less, and the Orangemen responded by moving more when Edelin ran set plays.

"Coach has been giving him time," Anthony said. "And all he really needed was an opportunity."

After the game, Edelin smiled as he greeted Frank, Erick and two other friends from home. Watching Edelin run the floor as he did so many days back in Maryland, Frank and Erick could barely tell their buddy had weathered a pair of suspensions and a year-and-a-half away from competitive basketball.

To them, he looked like Same Old Billy. ∎

JEREMY
MᶜNEIL

Height - 6-8 **Hometown** - San Antonio
Weight - 257 **High school** - Sam Houston

2002 – 2003
STATISTICS

GP-GS	MIN	PTS	FG PCT
35 - 0	18.8	3.3	.667

3FG PCT	REB	AST	BLK
.000	4.2	0.2	100

McNeil's blocks give him new outlook as SU moves to Sweet 16

BY CHRIS CARLSON | 3.25.03

BOSTON — It's remarkable what winning an NCAA Tournament game or two can do for your outlook.

A few weeks ago, Jeremy McNeil was moody, sullen and brooding. Questions about his play brought unprintable answers more often than not.

But after securing CBS's player of the game honor and helping the Syracuse men's basketball team to the Sweet 16 with four points and four blocks in a 68-56 win against Oklahoma State on Sunday, McNeil sported a grin.

For good reason, too. Without McNeil, Syracuse might be preparing for next season rather than Friday's game against Auburn in Albany.

"I just try to go out and play as hard as I can," McNeil said. "I don't want to let my teammates down."

McNeil's carefully chosen words were nothing compared to the volumes of praise his teammates heaped on him.

"They're coming at him like 100 miles per hour," forward Hakim Warrick said. "He's a freak of nature to be able to take hits like that. I'd try to take a charge or something."

Said Carmelo Anthony: "No. Hell no, I can't take those hits. Once he gets one block, everybody starts changing their shots. Some guys kept trying to dunk over (McNeil), but he kept getting them."

McNeil's teammates aren't guilty of exaggeration.

Down 17 points Sunday, Syracuse was forced to use a pressure defense against Oklahoma State. The Cowboys often broke through easily, swarming two or three players toward McNeil.

The first time the Cowboys came at him, McNeil had what looked like a clean block on center Andre Williams but was called for a foul.

"I thought Jeremy had a great block on the first block that they called a foul," SU head coach Jim Boeheim said. "Then he had a couple other blocks. When they got playing faster, they got out of their offense."

As the Oklahoma State offense sped up, it spent more time running into SU's brick wall.

Moments after the foul, guard Tony Allen attempted to dunk over McNeil. Although McNeil failed to get a piece of the ball, his body stopped Allen's momentum, and the ball flew off the backboard.

The stat sheet had McNeil finishing with four blocks, but he altered countless shots. He also started the second half for the first time this season, relegating Craig Forth to the bench.

"When one plays well, the other's upset because he doesn't," said associate head coach Bernie Fine, who works with the centers. "You just wish they both would."

During the past three games, in which McNeil has totaled 15 blocks, he's been the one playing well.

To see what McNeil means to SU's press, all you have to do is take him away. During two possessions with McNeil on the bench, the Cowboys broke out in transition. SU guard Josh Pace had the unenviable task of being the last man back. During his first attempt, Pace allowed Williams to dunk and then caught a knee to the face.

After leaving the game for three minutes, Pace returned and found himself in the same vulnerable position. With three Cowboys charging toward him, Williams plowed over Pace, while Ivan McFarlin converted the layup.

Fine said McNeil's impact has been two-pronged. As McNeil continues to block shots, his intimidating aura grows, making opponents hesitant about entering the lane.

More important, McNeil has begun to stop falling for head fakes. Although he still leaves the ground too often, he's improving, allowing him to stay out of foul trouble.

"I don't know how to take a charge," McNeil said. "I hope they keep coming into the lane. That way I can keep getting more blocks." ∎

JOSH PACE

| Height - 6-5 | Hometown - Griffin, Ga. |
| Weight - 190 | High school - Griffin |

GP-GS	MIN	PTS	FG PCT
32 - 0	14.7	4.3	.525
3FG PCT	**REB**	**AST**	**BLK**
.000	2.7	1.9	8

Pace's sleepy looks belie spark he provides off bench

BY CHRIS CARLSON | 12.3.03

Sometimes Josh Pace looks like he would rather be anywhere but on a basketball court.

His slow amble across the hardwood seems better suited for a crowded mall than a Syracuse men's basketball practice. His silent demeanor would fit in equally with librarians or teammates. His half-closed eyes — reminiscent of former NBA player Eric "Sleepy" Floyd — make him look more anxious to lay in bed than convert a layup.

But Pace, generously listed as a 6-foot-6 shooting guard, hasn't spent his time replenishing his energy by sleeping. Instead, he's been providing the Orangemen with an energy boost off the bench.

"When the time comes," Pace said, "I produce."

Chances are, things will be no different tonight when Syracuse (1-1) plays Colgate (2-2) at 7 in the Carrier Dome.

"(Pace) brings an intensity to our game," freshman point guard Gerry McNamara said. "We just feed off him. For him to give us that is more valuable than him giving us 30 points."

Pace has played more than 20 minutes in each of SU's first two games.

In the opener against Memphis, he jumpstarted a stagnant SU offense, making all five field goal attempts in a 70-63 loss. During an 81-66 win over Valparaiso on Nov. 24, he finished just 2 of 7, but the Orangemen built momentum with Pace on the floor.

The sophomore tallied four rebounds, six assists and a block with only two turnovers.

Against Memphis, Pace replaced an ineffective Kueth Duany at shooting guard. Against Valparaiso, SU head coach Jim Boeheim switched to a smaller lineup, using Pace and Duany together and benching centers Craig Forth and Jeremy McNeil. Pace also briefly spelled McNamara at point guard.

"He's like a Miami football player in terms of basketball," assistant coach Mike Hopkins said. "He's big enough to play (small forward), smart enough to play (point guard) and fast enough to play (shooting guard)."

Pace has flourished in the sixth-man role. He ranks fifth on SU in minutes and points, but is third in rebounds, second in assists and tied for first in steals.

"I would say he's very unusual in that regard," Boeheim said. "Most guys take more time to warm up. He comes right in and starts playing. Most guys struggle with that."

Pace insists this is nothing new. But last year, it appeared only in flashes.

Sure, Pace sparked the Orangemen to a Feb. 4 win over West Virginia with 12 points, five steals and five rebounds and also shot 4 of 6 against Richmond in the NIT quarterfinals on March 20.

But he barely saw the floor during early-season matchups with DePaul and Michigan State and failed to play a minute in two of Syracuse's first five Big East contests.

Pace struggled to adjust mentally from a high school star to a college reserve.

Worse yet, he was slotted behind Duany, sharpshooter Preston Shumpert, former point guard James Thues and DeShaun Williams.

"It was tougher last year," Pace said. "I was disappointed not playing as much as I thought I should, but it was something I had to do. In high school, I started all the time. Last year, I had to come off the bench."

Pace has been overshadowed at SU.

Last season, 7-footer Craig Forth's potential and Hakim Warrick's high-flying dunks earned fanfare among the freshmen. This year, newcomers McNamara and Carmelo Anthony earned starting spots. And next year, another top recruiting class should battle Pace for playing time.

All the while, Pace has refused to gripe about his sixth-man status.

"I just try to wait my turn," Pace said.

Neither Pace, nor his numbers, have to speak about his importance to Syracuse. His teammates will do that for him.

"He might get overlooked as far as the fans go," McNamara said. "But as far as I'm concerned, he's one of the most valuable members of this team." ∎

JIM
BOEHEIM

DOB - 11.17.1944 **Hometown** - Lyons N.Y.
Yrs. at SU - 27 **High school** - Lyons Central

STATISTICS

MEN'S COACH

RECORD	WIN PCT	AVG WINS
653-226	.742	25.2

NCAA TOURNAMENT

RECORD	WIN PCT	TITLES
38-21	.632	1

BY CHRIS CARLSON | 4.4.03

Everywhere you look, Jim Boeheim is there.

There he is rubbing elbows with Michael Wilbon and Tony Kornheiser on "Pardon the Interruption," making like the predictors and prognosticators he loves to bash. Now, he's on the radio from Bennigan's or ripping into author Murray Sperber on "SportsCenter."

If Boeheim's not on the air, chances are his gawky arms are contorting violently on the sideline or his bifocals are glaring at the officials about a foul call that they — and perhaps everybody besides Boeheim himself — missed out on.

It's hard to overlook Boeheim. He's everywhere, after all. But somehow the Naismith Board of Selectors did. Two days ago Kentucky's Tubby Smith was named Naismith College Coach of the Year.

"It's just unbelievable that people aren't talking about (Boeheim) as coach of the year," Syracuse assistant coach Mike Hopkins said before the announcement. "People talk about (freshmen) Carmelo Anthony, Gerry McNamara and all the talent. But to have these guys playing like they are at this time of year is just amazing."

Smith's a safe selection. He's safe like ordering a hamburger in an exotic restaurant or giving your dad a tie at Christmas. Just because it's safe doesn't make it right.

The award doesn't take the postseason into account, so ignore Kentucky's unexpected exit from the NCAA Tournament. Smith's Wildcats finished the season No. 1. They were the first team ever to move undefeated through the SEC regular season.

Kentucky started the year ranked No. 17. Five of 15 preseason publications that the SEC lists on its Web site had Kentucky among the top 10. Syracuse, meanwhile, is one of three teams currently in the top 15 that began the year unranked. Louisville and Creighton are the others.

Marquette's Tom Crean would have been more deserving than Smith. Same with Louisville's Rick Pitino.

Boeheim trumps them all.

"We weren't picked in the top 50 in the preseason," associate head coach Bernie Fine said. "We won the Big East West. We were the youngest team in the country all year."

Kentucky was led by three seniors — including bona fide superstar Keith Bogans — and three juniors. Three freshmen and a sophomore led the Orangemen.

Boeheim, though, would rarely admit their youth. Anthony, McNamara and Billy Edelin were always "mature freshmen" or "experienced freshmen" or "not your normal freshmen."

"He's never treated them like freshmen," Hopkins said. "The reality of it is he's treating these guys the way he treated (former SU standout) John Wallace in 1996."

When the freshmen did struggle, Boeheim rarely blamed them. Instead, he resorted to his usual suspects. Senior Kueth Duany — who's been Boeheim's whipping boy for four years — and junior Jeremy McNeil took more than their share of Boeheim's public tirades. The youngsters took their lumps in practice, not in the papers. Duany and McNeil could handle it.

Earlier in the year, McNamara might not have been able to. Until a breakout game March 4, against Notre Dame, McNamara struggled shooting on the road. As often as he could, Boeheim found others to blame.

If an unusually poor game forced Boeheim to criticize McNamara or Anthony, he didn't rip them like the other Orangemen. He matter-of-factly called them what they were.

"These two guys played like freshmen in the first half tonight," Boeheim said after SU struggled to a win in the second round of the NCAA Tournament against Oklahoma State.

Said Hopkins: "He's a good psychologist, he knows who he can push and he knows who he can't push."

Players praise Boeheim for letting them play. Boeheim forgets forward Hakim Warrick's fading jumpers when they aren't falling and ignores McNamara's occasional contested 3-pointer. Instead of pulling the plug on a player's night after an awkward shot, Boeheim allows them to continue.

In practice, he's allowed their youthful exuberance free reign. Stretching lines resemble stand-up acts. Layup drills turn into dunk contests. Smiles, jokes and wrestling matches are unchecked, as long as they don't interfere with the hour of serious practice Boeheim demands.

The lax discipline might not work with every team, but Boeheim's kids need their playtime.

"I'm more patient than I used to be," Boeheim said. "I don't get upset as easily."

Most impressively, though, Boeheim's handled any impending crisis with skill.

He weathered the rocky return of Edelin, allowing the point guard to miss the first 12 games of the year, work his way back slowly and eventually become one of the team's primary scorers.

He's kept Anthony, who may head to the NBA next year, focused on now rather than later.

"I'm biased," Fine said. "I think he should be Coach of the Year."

Sure you're biased. It doesn't mean you're wrong.

"I don't rate my seasons. You guys (the media) do a good…" Boeheim paused. "You guys do that for me."

This year, maybe Boeheim should have done it himself. The other guys didn't do such a good job. ■

Freshman Anthony scores 37 in Syracuse debut

STORY BY CHRIS CARLSON | PHOTOS BY BEN BLOKER

Carmelo Anthony glanced at an index card filled with goals before last night's exhibition contest against Nike Elite.

Five rebounds. One steal. Eight deflections.

Too bad there wasn't one for points. He might have doubled it.

Anthony scored 37 points, leading the Syracuse men's basketball team to a 93-74 win over Nike Elite in front of 6,330 at the Carrier Dome. And just for good measure, he met all the other goals as well.

"Unless you're deaf, blind and dumb, you have to be happy with his performance," Syracuse coach Jim Boeheim said. "We need other guys to step up."

Anthony scored as many points by himself as Nike Elite had in either half, shooting 14 of 22 from the field. And he did it quietly.

"How many did he have?" guard Josh Pace asked about the offensive outburst.

"Did he really?" questioned Gerry McNamara.

Anthony's most dominant run began at the start of the second half, when he reeled off seven straight points. He began the spree by converting a layup off a loose ball and followed that with a break-away dunk. The capper was a three-pointer over the head of a Nike Elite defender Exree Hipp. Later in the half, Anthony scored eight consecutive points for SU.

"He's one of those guys who can score any which way," freshman Billy Edelin said. "He's going to go inside. He'll find a three every now and then. After a while, the points stack up."

Against Nike Elite, Anthony stacked points by using every method. He finished 6 for 6 from the free-throw line, 3 for 8 on three-pointers and converted a pair of putbacks on five offensive rebounds. He had nine boards for the game.

Even Anthony wasn't sure of his totals after the contest.

"I didn't realize I scored that many points," Anthony said. "In my first college game, I'd say I met my goals. That's a pretty big accomplishment."

Boeheim, though, saw a negative to Anthony's dominant performance. Rather than run through their motion offense, the Orangemen watched Anthony. The result was a motion offense that was, at times, motionless.

Centers Craig Forth and Jeremy McNeil were victimized by the lack of movement, turning the ball over a combined seven times.

"Craig had four turnovers, but three of those weren't really his," Boeheim said. "We didn't really help him. That was a result of people not moving. People tended to let him do it all."

While the rest of the team failed to follow Anthony's example, Boeheim was impressed with the play of freshman Gerry McNamara. McNamara, who started at point guard, played conservatively during his 28 minutes, avoiding reckless drives into the lane while amassing four assists to no turnovers.

"I was a little conservative," McNamara said, "but I think I had to be in my first game. I didn't want to turn the ball over. As we get into the season, I'll show some of the other things I can do."

McNamara, who was told he would start on Monday night, also split time at point guard with Pace.

Pace, who also played at shooting guard, appeared equally adept at handling both positions, weaving his way into the lane and scoring 12 points on an assortment of floating jumpers.

Lost in the mix was Edelin, who played the fewest minutes, 17, among the guards. Edelin scored all six of his points in the second half after amassing only five minutes in the opening stanza.

"It was a toss-up between me and Billy," McNamara said. "We both worked hard in practice." ■

No Freebies: Anthony's missed foul shots doom SU

STORY BY CHRIS CARLSON | PHOTOS BY NATALIA JIMENEZ

NEW YORK CITY — As Carmelo Anthony missed his fifth consecutive free throw, he left his hand dangling in the air. He stood at the free-throw line, refusing to join his teammates in a scrum for the loose ball.

Anthony was tired. Tired from playing 40 minutes, scoring 27 points and carrying the Syracuse men's basketball team. And tired of missing free throws that cost Syracuse a chance to catch Memphis late in last night's 70-63 loss at Madison Square Garden.

"I was frustrated at the line," Anthony said. "I got down on myself. You're not supposed to be thinking about anything when you're shooting free throws."

The rest of the Orangemen were frustrated too. After the loss to a Memphis team that was missing two of its top five players because of suspensions, Syracuse players sat sullenly in the locker room.

Hakim Warrick pulled a headband over his eyes, while Josh Pace bowed his head. Kueth Duany harped away, encouraging Warrick to cheer up.

"We're not going to play 35 bad games," Duany told Warrick. "We played bad, they played good. You've got to keep your head up. I'm going to keep mine up."

Against Memphis, though, there was plenty to get down about. Starters Warrick, Duany and Craig Forth shot a combined 5 of 23, leaving freshman Gerry McNamara and Anthony to score 41 of SU's 63.

The Tigers answered the Orangemen's much ballyhooed pairing.

SEASON PLAY BY PLAY

With about five minutes to play, Syracuse led, 61-60, and Anthony had just drawn the fourth foul on Memphis center Earl Barron. Anthony stepped to the line and clanked the first two of his five clutch free-throw attempts.

After easily penetrating the Syracuse zone, sophomore Anthony Rice swished a floater to give Memphis the lead for good. The Tigers' fatal strike, though, came on the next sequence.

Anthony drove to the lane and was fouled by Rice again. And again, he choked on both free-throw attempts.

"Why do you think he missed the free throws?" Syracuse coach Jim Boeheim asked. "He was tired."

On the ensuing possession, Memphis freshman Jeremy Hunt drove down the right side of the lane, drew a bump from guard Josh Pace and dropped a floater into the basket. He converted the free throw and then buried two more on the following possession. Hunt's flurry was part of a 12-0 run that gave Memphis a 68-61 lead and put the game away.

Fellow freshman Rodney Carney (12 points) and senior John Grice (17 points) aided Hunt. Carney helped the Tigers to a 43-34 halftime lead, scoring all his points in the opening 20 minutes and snatching a team-high nine rebounds.

Anthony scored 21 of his 27 points in the first half, before receiving assistance from McNamara in the second. McNamara drained three three-pointers in the second stanza, helping Syracuse close the gap.

Syracuse's tandem, though, couldn't top Memphis' three equally inexperienced scorers.

"We have two good freshmen, and a third guy who's only played eight career games," Memphis coach John Calipari said. "I've been beating up on these guys for 25 days. I've been as hard on them as I have on anyone since I was 28 or 29 years old."

Calipari considers the third member of Memphis' scoring trio, Grice, almost equivalent to a freshman. Grice attended Southwest Tennessee Community College for two years and played eight games last year before being declared academically ineligible.

Calipari said he spent the preseason berating the inexperienced players in an effort to toughen them up.

"Grice is the one you should be talking about," Calipari said. "He's the real story."

Maybe so, but it was Hunt who had SU talking after the game.

"I hadn't really heard about him at all," Anthony said. "I didn't know who he was. He came through at the end though. He's a good player. Tonight, he hit his free throws." ■

Duany flops, SU follows in opener at the Garden

COLUMN BY ELI SASLOW

NEW YORK CITY — Plopped comfortably on the Syracuse bench, sitting three chairs from the scorer's table, SU's senior leader Kueth Duany repeatedly got up to help his teammates.

Six times in the second half, in fact, Duany jumped to the aid of younger Orangemen who dutifully refer to Duany as their mentor. After timeouts, as tired Orangemen walked to the bench, Duany eagerly jumped up to offer his seat.

That was about as big a contribution as he made in last night's 70-63 loss to Memphis at Madison Square Garden. He certainly did nothing on the court.

"I'm very disappointed in our veteran players," said Syracuse head coach Jim Boeheim of SU's two upper classmen, Duany and junior Jeremy McNeil. "They gave us basically nothing."

Duany actually may have given less than that. Syracuse's lone senior, Duany made just 3 of 9 shots. He failed to make any of his four attempts from three-point range. He had only four rebounds. He didn't have an assist.

For 21 painful minutes yesterday, Duany acted as dead weight to a young Syracuse team. Missed shot after missed shot, he sunk a team that, in the summer, he helped mold and build.

"I definitely feel like I let my team down tonight," Duany said. "I'm going to talk to them about it. I feel really awful. But I'm the leader, so I can't put my head down. I've got to take this as a challenge."

If his own disappointment doesn't serve as enough motivation, though, Boeheim offered plenty of challenges.

In the postgame press conference, Boeheim said he was "disappointed with the veterans" six times.

"The veterans didn't bring it," Boeheim said. "No excuse for that. It's just extremely disappointing. You can't show up and not be ready to play. I hope they learned that tonight."

Translation: Kueth, get your act together.

"That's just him issuing me a personal challenge," Duany said. "He likes to call me out a little bit. I don't take it personally. It seems like that's been happening every game since I stepped onto the Syracuse campus. But it doesn't bother me. He's just trying to help motivate me.

"The thing is, this team really needs me. I need to be the consistent guy in here. The steady guy."

Earlier this year, Syracuse coaches raved that Duany — plagued by inconsistency last year — had finally molded into that steady player. In practices, Duany's jump shot flew with more arc than in years past. It splashed through the net a little more often.

When Syracuse held an intrasquad scrimmage Nov. 2, Duany led the team in scoring. He slashed through the lane and made layups and recorded double-digit rebounds and hit the three and found open teammates. He looked poised for a quick start to the season.

"I came in here with a lot of confidence," Duany said. "I've been playing pretty well. I thought I'd have a fast start."

He thought he'd start the season like he did last year's campaign, when he averaged 20 points to lead Syracuse to the Preseason National Invitation Tournament title, also held in Madison Square Garden.

From there, though, Duany's 2001-02 season fell fast. He broke his nose, lost his outside shot and spent more time on the bench late in the year than Hakim Warrick, the sixth man.

Duany started last season well and progressively got worse. If that downward trend continues, his biggest role might continue to be giving up his seat during timeouts.

"This is just one game," Duany said. "I didn't shoot well. I'll get over it."

"He does a lot of things for us even if he's not playing well," guard Josh Pace said. "He can give us a boost emotionally. He's a big-time leader for us."

But for Syracuse to be successful, Duany will have to be more than that. He'll have to be a player, too. ■

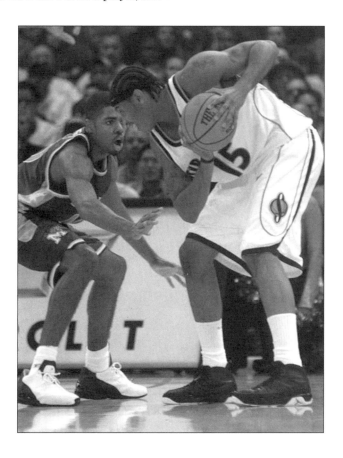

Orangemen work out kinks at point guard in exhibition

STORY BY PETE IORIZZO | PHOTOS BY AMY YOUNG

Call it the tale of two point guards.

The shooter, not surprisingly, sported his Syracuse men's basketball warmup suit and participated in the pregame shoot-around. He found his favorite spot outside the three-point arc, smoothly spotted up and swished a couple shots.

The slasher and passer, surprisingly, sat on the bench during that time. He almost receded into the first row of the stands because of his gray T-shirt and matching sweat pants.

The shooter, Gerry McNamara, poured in 13 points, including three threes, as Syracuse defeated Upstate New York AAU, 110-88, in an exhibition game at the Carrier Dome last night.

The quick cutter and skilled passer, Billy Edelin, never left the bench. Because last night's game was an exhibition, Edelin's NCAA-imposed 12-game suspension for playing in recreational-league games last winter did not apply. But the freshman decided not to play, anyway.

"Billy didn't want to play," Syracuse head coach Jim Boeheim said. "His comment was, 'Coach, these guys need to play.' I thought about playing him. I talked to Billy last night. He just thought it'd be better for the team. If it was a two-game suspension, like it should've been, he'd be playing."

So while Edelin sat, McNamara played 26 minutes at point guard, sharing time with Josh Pace, a shooting guard by trade.

McNamara complained of stiff legs early in the first half, and it showed in the first five minutes, when he committed a turnover and missed two three-pointers.

In fact, as a whole, Syracuse bumbled through much of the first half, looking uncoordinated and confused. At one point, Upstate NY AAU led, 28-26, and with 1:42 remaining, it trailed, 37-36.

In the second half, though, SU settled down, allowing McNamara more settled, open looks. He delivered, hitting 3 of his next 4 three-pointers.

"He's better when we can get him to spot-ups," Boeheim said, "and he doesn't have to make them off the dribble."

McNamara finished with eight assists, including an alley-oop feed to Hakim Warrick to cap the first half.

Plays like that, McNamara hopes, will help quash his reputation as simply a shooter. Some even suggest he'd make a better shooting guard.

"He's learning," said senior Kueth Duany, who rebounded from a poor performance against Memphis in the season opener with 22 points on 9-of-14 shooting. "Every day, he's improving. Every practice, he's just getting more comfortable at the point guard position. (He's) finding guys and getting his teammates the ball."

But what does he need to work on?

"Finding guys and getting his teammates the ball," Duany repeated.

Indeed, McNamara's eight assists trailed Pace's nine. Pace, who will join the point guard mix because of Edelin's suspension, took over the point when McNamara sat.

"It's a new position for me still," Pace said. "I've just got to get used to it. I'm going to be in the rotation. I'm just holding it down till Billy's back here."

Pace even made a few passes reminiscent of Edelin, winging the ball to a cutting Matt Gorman for a second-half layup that pushed the Syracuse lead to 75-62. Later, he dished to Gorman again, setting him up for a jumper that put the Orangemen ahead, 91-71.

"I think I played all right," Pace said. "I was just trying to get the team involved, get myself involved."

He did a better job getting the team involved. Pace struggled with his shot, hitting just 2 of 8, including a botched two-handed dunk late in the second half.

Although Pace played most of the 14 minutes McNamara spent on the bench at point guard, Boeheim said the two will probably not split time that evenly during the regular season.

For now, it's McNamara's team, with Pace as the first option off the bench.

"I came here to play basketball," McNamara said. "I wasn't thrown into anything. I didn't come here to sit on the bench. I came here to play, and right now, I'm playing." ∎

SU rips Valpo, Boeheim rips centers McNeil, Forth

STORY BY DARRYL SLATER | PHOTOS BY TRACY SIMPSON

On Sunday afternoon, Jim Boeheim delivered a frustrated message to struggling Syracuse men's basketball centers Craig Forth and Jeremy McNeil: If you don't play better, your team's not going to win.

In SU's 81-66 win over Valparaiso before 18,874 at the Carrier Dome, Forth, hampered by a sore right Achilles tendon, went scoreless and had two rebounds in 14 minutes. McNeil had zero points, five rebounds and five fouls in 19 minutes. Freshmen Carmelo Anthony and Gerry McNamara picked up the slack, scoring 28 and 18 points, respectively.

"Our centers are really struggling big-time," Boeheim said. "They've just got to get more productive for us to be effective."

When asked to detail Forth and McNeil's ineffectiveness, which forced the 6-foot-8 Hakim Warrick to play center, Boeheim said curtly, "We're playing a guy 195 pounds (Warrick) at center. I can't send a clearer message than that."

It appeared as though Boeheim was done, but he was just getting started.

"Jeremy was in perfect position a couple times to rebound," Boeheim said. "He's just glued to the floor. I constantly tell him, 'We'd like to play you more minutes.' But every time he plays 20 minutes, he's out of the game. On the first pass, we hit him with a perfect pass, and it took him so long to get up in the air, he couldn't get the shot off."

The coach then turned his attention to Forth, saying, "Craig has not really practiced well or played well. He's a limited jumper, and, now, he's not able to jump at all. His Achilles has been bothering him since August. He's got to have all the mobility that he's got to be effective."

Forth underwent an MRI on his Achilles, but the test showed no major problems, Boeheim said.

In the SU locker room after the game, Forth gingerly pulled on his socks and sneakers. When asked if the sore Achilles has hampered his mobility, Forth said "everything hampers my mobility" and slammed his locker door.

Later, Forth stood with his father, Murray, and team doctor Irving Raphael and discussed the nagging injury.

"He's battling through it," forward Kueth Duany said.

McNeil, meanwhile, slumped dejectedly in front of his locker as his teammates fielded questions from reporters. When asked about not finishing on open looks, he asked, "I was getting some open looks?"

When pressed for another question, he paused, shook his head and said, "I've got nothing to say. I'm not gonna point fingers. We won the game."

Said Duany: "This is one bad game for (Forth and McNeil). They've been playing well in practice. They just didn't come to play this afternoon."

On Sunday, Forth and McNeil were repeatedly victimized by the Crusaders' 6-foot-11 center Raitis Grafs, who had 18 points and eight rebounds. With 7:40 left in the first half, Grafs put Valpo up, 23-13, with a 12-foot jump shot in Forth's face. Boeheim called a timeout and benched Forth in favor of Warrick.

With about 13 minutes left in the second half, Forth returned to a chorus of boos from the student section and barely touched the ball on offense before Boeheim yanked him again at the 9:47 mark.

Then, with 5:44 remaining and SU leading, 59-55, McNeil fouled out, but Boeheim chose to move Warrick to center rather than reinsert Forth. Warrick scored just two points over the next 3:26, but the

Orangemen went on an 11-2 run to seal the game.

"I knew it was going to be tough (playing center)," Warrick said. "I just wanted to go out there and hold down the middle, play tough and not let them get easy shots."

When Duany fouled out with 2:16 remaining, Forth returned, this time to louder boos from the students. Within 30 seconds, Forth committed a foul, and Boeheim screamed in the center's direction again.

"We've got a way to go before we can even think about being a good basketball team," Boeheim said. "And it's not really the guard play as much as it is getting something more done inside. We've got to do better inside, there's no question about that." ∎

Orangemen's defense shaky in blowout of Colgate

STORY BY CHRIS CARLSON | PHOTOS BY MONICA PADLUCK

Kueth Duany searched the bleachers for somebody who would understand what happened to the Syracuse men's basketball team's defense.

During a break late in the second half last night, he made eye contact with former SU point guard Allen Griffin and offered a quick assessment.

"Too many open threes," he mouthed repeatedly.

Despite the margin of victory, the 98-68 victory over Colgate at the Carrier Dome was as much cause for postgame concern as for celebration.

The Raiders (2-3) stuck close to the Orangemen (2-1) in the first half by burying 8 of 13 three-pointers. Colgate led by a bucket, 46-44, with less than two minutes remaining in the first half before SU used a 10-1 run for a 54-47 halftime lead.

"It was awful," point guard Gerry McNamara said of the defense.

"It was non-existent," Duany said. "There were way too many open shots."

Colgate's barrage of threes began after SU led 41-30 with 4:45 left in the first.

Carmelo Anthony lost track of Colgate senior Tim Sullivan, who buried a three from the corner. Then, on consecutive possessions, guard Alvin Reed pulled up and nailed three-pointers before McNamara could put a hand in his face. Sullivan completed the streak by hitting another long-distance attempt.

"It was like a bad dream we couldn't get up from," SU forward

Hakim Warrick said. "We just made things harder for ourselves. If you had told me before the game that would happen, I'd have said you were crazy or something."

While Warrick couldn't believe Colgate's early shooting, other Orangemen weren't surprised. McNamara played high school basketball against Colgate guard Mark Linebaugh, who made 1 of 2 three-point attempts.

"You get a lead on a team and then you think you can coast," McNamara said. "We knew they had some shooters."

But the foresight helped neither he nor Anthony, who left Sullivan wide open on all three of Sullivan's three-pointers in the first half.

SU head coach Jim Boeheim estimated the freshmen each made 10 to 15 defensive mistakes in the first half and Colgate converted most into scoring opportunities.

"They don't give up a basket for every one they get, but they try to sometimes," Boeheim said.

Not all the blame, though, can be placed on Anthony and McNamara. They played the most minutes of any Orangeman (34 and 33, respectively) and, as usual, carried the offensive load.

For the third consecutive game, Anthony led Syracuse in scoring, compiling 20 of his 27 points in the first half — including 15 in the first eight minutes. McNamara, meanwhile, finished with 14 points — including 4 of 6 three-point attempts — and a tidy six assists with no turnovers.

"My main concern is that they're spending so much energy on offense that there is a diminishing amount of energy you have left," Boeheim said. "No one admits they're getting tired, but Carmelo is getting tired."

Syracuse's defense improved in the second half with a return to its traditional 2-3 zone. In the first half, Boeheim refused to abandon the man-to-man defense.

In the second half, he switched between a press, zone and man-to-man coverage. Colgate shot 2 of 14 on three-pointers against a variety of defenses and was held scoreless in the final six minutes.

"Our zone's been good in every game we played," Boeheim said. "That's a positive sign."

"The zone helped a little bit," Duany said. "I'd like to say it was the defense. We picked up our intensity a little bit in the second half, but they lost some of their juice as well."

With Colgate tiring, the Orangemen ran their in-state opponent out of the Dome, outscoring the Raiders, 44-21, in the second half.

Still, the late firepower and margin of victory weren't enough to appease SU.

"We're just not there yet," Boeheim said. "We're a long way from where we need to be." ∎

SEASON PLAY BY PLAY

McNeil savors blocks against helpless Raiders

STORY BY PETE IORIZZO

The motion Jeremy McNeil makes when he swings his right arm forward in an apparent attempt to swat the basketball into the fifth row can only be described one way.

"Oh it's violent," Syracuse assistant coach Mike Hopkins said. "It's violent and it's hard. It's very hard."

"When I block a shot," McNeil said, "it's like, 'OK, I'm ready.' That and when I dunk."

But after a violent block, McNeil turns surprisingly docile. The big man flashes an innocent smile after a job well done.

"He just gets the big smile," forward Hakim Warrick said, "and he starts having fun out there."

Last night, in Syracuse's 98-68 win over Colgate at the Carrier Dome, McNeil had plenty of reason to show his boyish grin. He blocked six Raider shots while playing 22 minutes, including most of the second half.

Playing against a relatively small Colgate lineup — starting center Andrew Zidar is 6 feet, 8 inches — McNeil allowed Raider forwards to catch the ball in the paint but then threw it back in their faces when they attempted layups.

"What I'm concerned about is, against bigger guys, he can't let them catch the ball," Syracuse head coach Jim Boeheim said. "Against these guys, he could let them catch the ball and still block the shot."

"I don't know how many blocks he had," Warrick said, "but

they started second-guessing coming in the hole after he got his first couple of blocks."

McNeil's first fierce block came late in the first half. When 6-foot-1 Colgate guard Alvin Reed attempted a layup, McNeil whacked the ball out of bounds toward the SU student section.

Craig Forth started the second half at center, but McNeil checked in four minutes later. He got a piece of a Zidar putback soon after and then swatted him again on the next Colgate possession.

"McNeil likes to block everything," Zidar said, "so we just wanted to get off the ground."

McNeil took to the air later in the second half. He became a rebounding force and converted several two-handed dunks that roused the announced crowd of 15,615. He finished with 12 points and seven rebounds on 5-of-7 shooting.

NO SHOW

Syracuse point guard Billy Edelin, who is serving an NCAA-imposed 12-game suspension for playing in an unsanctioned recreational league last winter, was not on the SU bench during the game. He also missed practice Monday.

According to the terms of Edelin's suspension, he is allowed to practice with the team and sit on the bench during games. He was on the bench during Syracuse's home opener against Valparaiso on Nov. 24.

Teammates Carmelo Anthony and Warrick said Edelin did not attend because he was busy with extra-credit school work.

WALK ON

With his team ahead by nearly 30 points, Boeheim decided to throw Colgate a different look late in the second half.

Actually, he threw the crowd a new look, too, considering not one of the five SU players on the court when time expired had

appeared in a regular-season game this season.

With 1:31 remaining, Boeheim sent Josh Brooks and Gary Hall onto the court to play with Ronneil Herron, Andrew Kouwe and Tyrone Albright. The all-walk-on lineup managed a point — Herron converted a free throw — while holding the Raiders scoreless.

In fact, Syracuse held Colgate scoreless for the final six minutes. For 3:14 of that time, at least one walk-on was in the game.

"I guess they did a pretty good job," senior Kueth Duany said.

"It was exciting," Warrick said. "Especially since Kouwe is one of my roommates. Seeing him out there, it's just great. I'm just waiting for them to score some baskets."

They almost did. After Albright created a turnover, he and Herron came in two- on-one, but both missed layups.

"They were a little nervous out there," Warrick said. "They come into practice, and they give us a run sometimes. We know they can play."

THIS AND THAT

Although Syracuse shot 62.5 percent from the free-throw line, including 50 percent (7 of 14) in the first half, Boeheim seemed unconcerned. "Overall, I don't think we've been a bad free throw shooting team. We're not going to be an 80-percent free-throw shooting team, but we'll be all right." Anthony, who led the Orangemen with 27 points, finished 5 of 9 from the charity stripe. ... With last night's win, Syracuse pushed its winning streak against Colgate to 37 games. The teams have met 155 times, with Syracuse holding a 110-45 advantage. The Raiders last topped the Orangemen in 1962, winning, 67-63. ... SU outrebounded Colgate, 43-40. Anthony led all rebounders with 11. ... Freshman Matt Gorman, who didn't play Nov. 24 against Valparaiso, played 12 minutes and had two points last night. ... With 11:54 remaining in the first half, all fans sitting in the upper deck were invited to move down to the lower level to fill the numerous empty seats. On nights when attendance is sparse this season, SU will make similar accommodations, said Michael Veley, Syracuse's associate athletics director for external affairs. "We have to be sensitive to the people who paid a lot to sit down here," Veley said, "but I saw a lot of season ticket holders applauding when the announcement was made." ∎

Cornell overwhelmed by Warrick's athleticism

STORY BY CHRIS CARLSON | PHOTOS BY NATALIA JIMENEZ

Hakim Warrick knew it was over when he stepped on the court. Josh Pace knew well before that.

Both Pace and Warrick figured that the Syracuse men's basketball team would dominate Cornell athletically long before the final buzzer of SU's 85-62 victory.

"You just sensed a mismatch," Warrick said. "You just sensed they couldn't match us athletically."

Warrick is the best example of the Orangemen's athletic advantage.

A beanpole of a power forward, Warrick's 6-foot-8 frame — which plays more like 6-foot-11 considering the length of his arms — stood 2 inches taller than Cornell power forward Grant Harrell, who attempted to guard him. Warrick ran the court as quickly as any Cornell guard, and jumped about as high as two CU players put together.

"He's just too big and too quick for these guys," Boeheim said. "He should have a good game against these guys.

The Big Red never found a way to counter the Orangemen's athleticism, as Warrick converted 9 of 13 shot opportunities and scored a season-high 20 points. Warrick's scoring display featured an array of awe-inspiring moves.

On the game's first basket, he backed down Harrell, spun, and leapt toward the Carrier Dome roof, reaching over Harrell and dropping the ball into the basket. Two possessions later, he snared a poor pass with one outstretched hand before repeating the same move.

SEASON PLAY BY PLAY

To see Hakim take off from the free-throw line like that is amazing. He might be the best dunker from the Big East.

KUETH DUANY
SU GUARD

Later in the game he'd bring the crowd to its feet — and Cornell to its knees — by making three steals and leaping from the free-throw line to complete three identical breakaway dunks.

Warrick's first dunk punctuated a 12-2 run that allowed Syracuse to take a 19-14 lead it never relinquished. Minutes later, a second slam highlighted a 9-3 run, leaving the score 28-17.

"To see Hakim take off from the free-throw line like that is amazing," senior Kueth Duany said. "He might be the best dunker from the Big East."

While Warrick insists he has added a short-range jump shot to his arsenal, he hasn't shown it yet, and didn't need to against Cornell.

"I'm not going to go out there and shoot 1,000 jump shots when I can have a layup every time," Warrick said. "If it's there and they're just giving it to me, I'll take it."

That was a good thing for the Orangemen, who received poor shooting performances from freshmen Carmelo Anthony and Gerry McNamara and senior Kueth Duany.

Syracuse's top three scorers shot a combined 13-of-35, although Anthony led the team in scoring for the fourth time in four games with 21 points.

"This was the first game we shot the ball poorly," Boeheim said. "Fortunately we did enough things to win, but we don't want to have too many games where they shoot like this."

Despite the height and athleticism advantages, Syracuse never buried Cornell. Early in the second half, Syracuse's defense — which was much improved from its win over Colgate — relaxed and allowed guard Cody Toppert to nail three straight three-pointers to cut the lead to nine during a 13-point second-half run.

"We knew he was their best shooter, and we didn't get out on him," Duany said. "We can't let one guy single-handedly dominate us. It's just effort. We didn't make the effort to go out there and get him."

The Orangemen held the Big Red to 9 of 30 on three-point attempts, including 2 of 12 in the first half.

SU was frustrated by its inability to dominate Cornell on the boards. The Orangemen were outrebounded, 16-14, on the offensive glasss by the not-so-Big Red. Rather than rely on technique, the Orangemen tried to use their athletic ability on the glass.

"We knew we had more talent coming into the game," Pace said. "But there's still things we need to work on. We weren't boxing out, we were trying to just jump over them." ■

SU continues hot play in romp over UNC-Greensboro

STORY BY CHRIS CARLSON | PHOTOS BY ZACK SECKLER

Hakim Warrick claims he's always had these moves.

He's always used the spin move that leaves even the most nimble forward guarding thin air. He's got an array of twists, turns and pivots that send defenders leaping toward the Carrier Dome ceiling while Warrick slides past.

Last night, Warrick displayed each one of his low-post maneuvers in front of 16,941, as Syracuse downed UNC-Greensboro, 92-65.

"I'm doing a better job of being aggressive," Warrick said. "I'm making my shots now, quick spins, short turnarounds. I came in with it last year, and no one really saw it. I had to wait my turn last year. This year I get to showcase that stuff."

Warrick's teammates fared well, too. Warrick led four Orangemen in double figures with a career-high 23 points — 16 in the first half — and contributed to Syracuse's most convincing and complete win of the season. Carmelo Anthony (22 points), Gerry McNamara (17 points) and Kueth Duany (11 points) also scored in double digits. Last night marked the first time Carmelo Anthony failed to lead SU in scoring.

It was also the second consecutive game Warrick dominated a physically inferior opponent. In wins over Greensboro and Cornell, Warrick shot a combined 19 of 27. But while he dominated on dunks against the Big Red, he used an assortment of low-post moves on the Spartans.

While Syracuse played well offensively throughout, the defense kicked in with 4:58 left in the first half. With the game tied, 32-32, the

Orangemen went on a 10-0 run on their way to a 45-35 halftime lead.

During the final five minutes, the Orangemen (4-1) held the Spartans (3-4) to three points. SU also forced four turnovers, recorded three of its 12 steals and tallied eight points in transition during that span.

"At certain points of the game we really got after it," McNamara said. "We always play good offensively. The key is defense. The defensive intensity wasn't there the whole game, but at certain points we had that intensity."

Warrick ignited the run by backing into the lane and elevating over the Spartans' defense for a layup. Moments later, Jeremy McNeil converted one of SU's four short-range transition baskets. Duany forced a timeout with another steal and breakaway slam at 3:50.

Warrick's final contribution to the run came two possessions later as he backed down a Greensboro defender and quickly spun to his right, leaving his opponent gawking at his heels before finishing with a slam.

"Offensively we have a chance to be very good," Syracuse head coach Jim Boeheim said. "Four guys in double figures should be enough most nights. Our defense is going to decide how good we can be."

Syracuse's defense, which has been a constant complaint of Boeheim's in the first four games, continued to fare well in the second half, holding the Spartans to 33 percent shooting, including 25 percent from three-point range.

Still, Boeheim, whose satisfaction before Big East play would constitute a 10th Wonder of the World, found fault with SU's defense.

Carmelo Anthony allowed a pair of uncontested alley-oops to senior James Maye, who led Greensboro with 19 points. The Orangemen allowed the Spartans to shoot 56 percent in the first half.

"If we had played poorly offensively, this game would have been down to the wire," Boeheim said. "The first half we played our zone, and they scored every possession. Then we switched to man, and they still scored. Our offense is good but, we still need to get better on the other end."

Still, the Orangemen blew out Greensboro — whom Boeheim called a future NCAA tournament team — by 27 points.

They dominated in all aspects. They forced 20 turnovers while losing eight. They totaled nine more blocks and nine more rebounds than their overmatched opponents.

"This is the best defensive game we played this year," Warrick said. "Offensively, we've played better but not against a strong a team as this. I'd say this was the most complete game this year." ∎

SEASON PLAY BY PLAY

Syracuse storms out of the gate to bury Binghamton

STORY BY DARRYL SLATER

For about 10 minutes Saturday night, Al Walker patrolled the Carrier Dome sidelines with vigor. The Binghamton men's basketball team followed its coach, fighting Syracuse for every rebound and playing scrappy defense.

The Orangemen quickly put a halt to the Bearcats' fury, jumping out to a 21-point lead in the opening 12:15 and earning a dominating 94-58 win before 19,770.

"Since we haven't been playing well in the beginning (of games)," SU forward Kueth Duany said, "we've focused especially on coming out and taking their heart in the beginning."

Syracuse freshman Carmelo Anthony scored 11 points in the first 12:15 and ended with 24 points, 11 rebounds and five assists, all game highs.

Anthony gave the Orangemen a 34-15 lead with 9:35 left in the first half when he shook off Binghamton's Brandon Carter and nailed a three-pointer in Carter's face. Earlier, Anthony jammed home a Hakim Warrick missed free throw.

"Coming out tonight, I tried to get everybody involved," said Anthony, who collected four assists and attempted two behind-the-back passes in the first half. "They came out and tried to run with us, but that's our game right there, and they couldn't beat us with our game."

The Orangemen found their hot hands early, shooting 67.7 percent in the first half. Anthony, Warrick and Duany, who's worked especially hard on shooting in practice this year, combined to

He stuffed a Binghamton player so hard that the sound of McNeil's hand smacking the ball could be heard across the court. The block seemed thunderous enough to flatten the ball, which seems fitting, considering the way the Orangemen deflated the Bearcats' hopes.

shoot 15 of 19 in the first 20 minutes.

"We were sharp right from the beginning," SU head coach Jim Boeheim said. "Tonight, everything was really just going in for us."

The Bearcats fought back, cutting the defecit to 52-36 at halftime. But the Orangemen went on a 20-8 run in the second half, capped by a two-handed Duany slam off Anthony's feed with 11:22 left.

Early in the second half, the Orangemen got a scare when Anthony tried an up-and-under layup and landed awkwardly on his right knee. The Dome crowd fell silent as the freshman writhed in pain, and SU doctors helped him to the locker room. Icing his bruised knee, Anthony returned a minute later to applause.

"When he went down, I heard him scream and say something about his knee," Warrick said. "But when he got up and was walking, I knew he was going to be fine."

Riding the early lead, the Orangemen mixed things up against the under-matched Bearcats late, even experimenting with a full-court press — with mixed results.

SU center Jeremy McNeil fed on Binghamton's small lineup, camping out underneath the basket to block five shots. McNeil closed the first half with a flurry of swats.

"If people challenge him, he's going to block shots," Boeheim said. "That's what he does."

Earlier, he stuffed a Binghamton player so hard that the sound of McNeil's hand smacking the ball could be heard across the court. The block seemed thunderous enough to flatten the ball, which seems fitting, considering the way the Orangemen deflated the Bearcats' hopes.

"It's really important to jump on them from the start," Warrick said, "and just keep rolling them throughout the game." ∎

SEASON PLAY BY PLAY

Syracuse proves its for real, pastes Georgia Tech

STORY BY CHRIS CARLSON | PHOTOS BY AMY YOUNG

During Friday's practice, Syracuse men's basketball coach Jim Boeheim made a threat to his team — a loss to Georgia Tech would mean the Orangemen would lose their right to go home for Christmas break.

After Saturday's 92-65 victory over the Yellow Jackets, Hakim Warrick said he thought Boeheim's threat was a joke. But then he paused and admitted he didn't know if Boeheim would have followed through.

Senior Kueth Duany, who has known Boeheim the longest, believed the threat was more than idle chatter.

"He said it before practice, and we knew we had to pick it up," Duany said. "We all had our bags packed before the game. We knew if we won we were going home."

For the first two minutes, it seemed like Duany would be spending his holidays in Syracuse rather than in Bloomington, Ind. But Duany's steal and breakaway dunk began a 21- 5 run that allowed the Orangemen to turn a 6-0 deficit into a blowout-to-be by halftime.

"The defense started it all," Warrick said. "The open looks we got, the transition game. That's what got us going."

Duany's defense may have provided the spark, but it was Gerry McNamara who torched the Yellow Jackets. McNamara drained three three-pointers during the run, scoring 16 of his 25 points in the first half.

"Every shot he shoots I think it's going in," Duany said. "When he shoots, I just start running back looking for someone to guard because I know it's cash."

McNamara did more than light up the nets. After McNamara hit three consecutive three-pointers, the Georgia Tech defense began darting toward McNamara as soon as he caught the ball. McNamara consistently sidestepped the on-rushing defenders and drove into the lane. He dished out eight of his 10 assists in the first half.

After the game, Boeheim said McNamara — who now leads SU in assists and three-point shooting — had not played close to his potential until Saturday.

"I don't think he's played up to his capabilities this year, as good as he's played," Boeheim said. "He's been one of the best freshmen in the country, and he hasn't played where he can play. He's used to scoring. He's had to scale back his game. Tonight he didn't scale anything back."

McNamara's handled Georgia Tech's full-court pressure defense. Rather than lose the ball, the Orangemen lost defenders, converting eight layups or dunks within a 14-minute span in the first half. During a 14-minute stretch, the Orangemen outscored the Yellow Jackets, 40-12.

McNamara's penetration allowed Duany to star as well. Duany took advantage of a number of wide-open opportunities, knocking down 6 of 7 first-half field-goals and both his three-point efforts. Duany didn't miss a shot until the final minute of the first half, and Syracuse shot 54.5 percent (24 of 44) in the first stanza.

"We couldn't miss," McNamara said. "It must have been fun to watch. We just made shot after shot."

Duany was also the catalyst in Syracuse's top defensive effort so far. The Yellow Jackets turned the ball over 19 times.

"We couldn't play both ends of the court any better," Boeheim said. "The second half of the game was almost anti-climactic. It was almost like we should just go home now. It was about as good as it's going to get."

With 6:28 to play in the first half, McNamara found Duany spotting

up for a three. After giving SU a 29-16 lead, Duany bellowed while McNamara shrugged smugly with satisfaction.

A little more than six minutes later, Carmelo Anthony drained a fade-away three-pointer at the buzzer, giving Syracuse a 58-25 half-time lead. Syracuse buried a season-best 10 three-pointers in the first half and finished 11 of 26.

"They had it going," Georgia Tech coach Paul Hewitt said. "When a guy makes a step-back three, you have to give it to him. We didn't react well to the run in the first half. They made shots. Sometimes this game is like that." ■

Syracuse crushes Albany

STORIES BY DARRYL SLATER | PHOTOS BY SETH SIDITSKY

Records fell in the Syracuse men's basketball team's 109-79 win over Albany on Dec. 28 at the Carrier Dome.

SU head coach Jim Boeheim earned his 630th career win. The Orangemen's 109 points were their most in 12 years. And SU center Jeremy McNeil recorded five blocks, moving him into seventh place on SU's all-time list, with 142.

The Orangemen outrebounded the Great Danes, 50-18, though no SU player had double-digit rebounds. Four Orangemen scored in double figures. Carmelo Anthony scored 28 points, Hakim Warrick had 22, Kueth Duany had 14 and Gerry McNamara tallied 11.

Jamar Wilson led Albany with 29 points.

Canisius hangs close to SU

A feisty Canisius squad gave the Syracuse men's basketball team more than it bargained for, but the Orangemen pulled away and pulled off an 87-69 win on Dec. 30 at the Carrier Dome.

The Golden Griffins led, 38-37, at halftime, but SU rattled off a 17-point run late in the second half, securing the win.

Hakim Warrick led SU with 25 points, and Carmelo Anthony added 23. Anthony also shot 10 of 12 on free throws. After shooting 50 percent in the first half, Canisius cooled and shot 36.4 in the second half. The Orangemen, meanwhile, shot 63.6 percent in the second half.

With Anthony on bench, Syracuse slips by Seton Hall

STORY BY PETE IORIZZO | PHOTOS BY SAED HINDASH (THE STAR LEDGER)

EAST RUTHERFORD, N.J. — Give the guys in Vegas this scenario.

Syracuse trails Seton Hall by six points with 7:59 remaining, and SU head coach Jim Boeheim has to relegate super-stud freshman Carmelo Anthony, who has just been slapped with his fourth foul, to the bench.

Boeheim knew what the Vegas boys would say: Bet the house on the Pirates.

"If you had to evaluate our chances when Carmelo Anthony got his fourth," Boeheim said, before pausing, "I'd say they were not good."

But fueled by stud freshman No. 2 Gerry McNamara and senior Kueth Duany, the Orangemen fired off an improbable 16-9 run during the next five minutes and escaped their Big East opener at Continental Airlines Arena with a 70-66 victory in front of 8,415 fans.

Many of those spectators wearing blue and white left howling at the officials. Syracuse (9-1, 1-0 Big East) held a 68-66 lead with 14.2 seconds remaining, but the Pirates (5-6, 0-2) had possession. Guard John Allen fed Andre Sweet, who along with Kelly Whitney had punished the Orangemen in the paint all game, under the basket. In traffic, Sweet appeared to be fouled and lofted an errant shot.

The whistle never sounded, and McNamara secured the rebound. He added two free throws to ice the game.

"There were some unbelievable calls," Boeheim said. "I don't want to hear about the last call. You've got to overcome calls, and we overcame horrendous calls."

Four foul calls, some questionable, forced Anthony to the bench for a 4:45 span in the second half. But McNamara swung the game with his defense and perimeter shooting.

He hit one three to close the Pirates' lead to 53-50 and then followed a Seton Hall basket with another three to pull Syracuse to within two.

McNamara attempted his third consecutive three-pointer on the following possession. Although he misfired, he drew a foul from Allen and hit all three free throws, giving him nine straight points and tying the game, 56-56.

"McNamara's tough," Seton Hall head coach Louis Orr said. "He's not your typical point guard, because he can shoot the ball. If he moves off the ball, he's still a threat to score."

On the next possession, Orr found out McNamara's a threat on defense, too. Despite having gone against physical guard Andre Barrett for the previous 35 minutes, McNamara mustered enough energy to play an aggressive press.

He picked off a pass and fed Kueth Duany, who soared through the paint for a one-handed dunk that gave SU a lead it would never relinquish. When Anthony returned with 3:14 left, the Orangemen led, 63-62.

"I think the steal was the turning point," said McNamara, who finished with 17 points on 4-of-8 shooting. "It fired us up, and it gave us a lift."

"I just got open shots, and I made them," said Duany, who led SU with 20 points and hit 6 of 8 shots. "There's nothing special about it. I don't remember plays. The play I remember was when the final buzzer went off."

Long before that, in the first half, it appeared Syracuse's porous defense would allow Seton Hall to secure its first Big East win. The Pirates put together a 16-2 run in the first half, scoring points in transition and taking advantage of SU's centers and forwards.

The Pirates grabbed nine first-half offensive rebounds and outscored

Syracuse, 22-12, in the paint. They also totaled seven fast-break points, while SU managed none.

Syracuse stayed in the game, trailing only 35-31 at halftime, mostly thanks to Anthony, who scored 16 of his 18 points in the first half. During the first 20 minutes, no other SU player collected more than five.

"They were trying to mix it up (on defense in the second half)," Anthony said. "I slowed down on offense. I had almost all of our points in the first half."

Luckily for Anthony and the Orangemen, McNamara and Duany scored 30 of SU's 39 second-half points.

"The game really turned on (Duany) and Gerry, when 'Melo went out with us down six," Boeheim said. "Our pressure got us just enough." ∎

100%
80%
60%
40%

35%

CARMELO-METER

A GAME-BY-GAME INDICATION OF CARMELO ANTHONY'S PERFORMANCE

Anthony had an off night, hitting 5 of 9 shots for 11 points in 26 minutes.

BIG NUMBER =

10

Blocks by Syracuse. Carmelo Anthony led SU with four, followed by Jeremy McNeil with three, Hakim Warrick with two and Craig Forth with one.

Whistles dominate as SU knocks off Boston College

STORY BY PETE IORIZZO | PHOTOS BY SETH SIDITSKY

As the Carrier Dome scoreboard clock ticked toward zero, a fan walking behind the Syracuse bench turned and hurled insults at Craig Forth so loudly that a few players and coaches turned around.

Remarkably, the referees did not whistle the foul-mouthed fan for a technical foul.

Their whistles did, however, scream 47 other times to signal personal-foul calls and twice more to dole out technicals — one to Syracuse men's basketball head coach Jim Boeheim and another to Boston College forward Andrew Bryant.

The latter allowed Syracuse to connect on four straight free throws that turned a slow, ugly game, which the Orangemen finally won last night, 82-74, in front of 20,692.

"I was scared to jump," said SU center Jeremy McNeil, one of four Syracuse players to finish with four personal fouls. "All I can do is stand there, or else they call a foul."

The referees did that 31 times in the second half. For Syracuse, in addition to McNeil, Hakim Warrick, Josh Pace and Carmelo Anthony also collected a quartet of fouls. Forth fouled out with almost 13 minutes remaining, and with 14 minutes left, the Orangemen had already collected their seventh team foul.

But time after time, Boston College, which shot 57 percent from the free-throw line, failed to capitalize. Worse, at the most crucial juncture, the Eagles allowed the Orangemen to shoot too many free throws.

After BC used a 16-2 run to take a five-point lead with 10:24 remaining in the second half, Bryant fouled Anthony to give SU the ball. He then committed another foul on the inbound pass. As he barked about the call, seemingly to no one in particular, the referee docked him with a technical.

McNamara hit the two free throws from the technical, and Anthony followed by converting both shots on a one-and-one to close the score to 59-58. The Eagles never recovered, as Syracuse went on to not only snatch the lead but also stretch it to 73-62 with 3:36 left.

"We should've played through it, but I felt (Bryant's technical) shouldn't have been called," said Boston College forward Craig Smith, who finished with 26 points but fouled out with 1:19 left. "(Bryant) wasn't talking to the ref. He was talking to himself. It shouldn't have been called."

Boeheim felt the same about his technical, which he picked up a little more than three minutes into the second half. The coach was whistled when he protested what appeared to be a soft call on Forth.

"I haven't got a technical in so long I can't remember," Boeheim said. "Craig didn't move. It was a horrible call. I said, 'What's that?' That's not a technical. That was horrible."

Fortunately for Boeheim, his team's free-throw shooting was not as horrible as the Eagles'. Although SU finished 65 percent from the line, it made 7 of 8 down the stretch as Boston College fouled in desperation.

Warrick hit five of his last six free throws, and McNamara, who has not missed in his last 30 free-throw attempts, went 4 for 4.

"This season, from the beginning, we've been criticized for free throws," said McNamara, who posted 20 points despite being guarded by BC star guard Troy Bell. "But the last two games, we've put the game away from the free-throw line."

It was almost over well before that, as Syracuse grabbed a big lead early and appeared poised to run away. After BC led, 4-3, Syracuse went on a 13-0 run. Thanks in part to the Eagles hitting just 9 of their first 25 shots, the Orangemen pushed their lead to 40-25.

A 7-0 Boston College run closed the score to 40-32 at halftime and set up the second-half comeback. But 16 missed three throws clipped the Eagles.

"(Free-throw shooting) has been a problem for us all year," BC head coach Al Skinner said. "If we made our free throws, it's a different game. But we're not a good free-throw shooting team." ∎

SEASON PLAY BY PLAY

Balancing act helps 'Cuse down No. 11 Missouri

COLUMN BY CHRIS CARLSON | PHOTOS BY SETH SIDITSKY

Gerry McNamara doesn't like to think of himself as solely a shooter.

At the beginning of the season, he cringed when constantly questioned about his 3-point shot. Despite hours of shooting practice, the self-professed gym rat insisted he brought more than an accurate outside shot.

During a 76-69 victory over No. 11 Missouri last night in front of 18,756 at the Carrier Dome, McNamara showcased his overall game and Syracuse showed off a well-balanced attack as all of its starters scored in double-figures.

McNamara finished with seven assists and four steals to go along with 14 points.

"Sometimes, we're spoiled by him," Syracuse head coach Jim Boeheim said. "He plays like a senior, and we expect him to play like a grad student. He's not perfect. By next week, he probably will be."

Leading by 13 points with 11 minutes left, the No. 25 Orangemen (11-1) dozed off, allowing the Tigers (10-2) a 9-0 run in a three-minute span. That forced Boeheim to expend a timeout and question whether his team was too tired to weather the explosion.

After the timeout, McNamara took over.

He got Syracuse off the schneid, burying a 3-pointer. On the following possession, he whistled a no-look pass to Hakim Warrick, who was fouled attempting a dunk. After Warrick made a free throw, McNamara buried a second 3-pointer, prompting freshman Carmelo Anthony to drape himself on McNamara's shoulders.

"We know McNamara's a good player," Missouri coach Quin Snyder said. "He showed a lot of poise out there tonight."

Despite his late sharpshooting, McNamara's normal accuracy was missing in the first half. Although he scored eight of his 14 points in the first 20 minutes, McNamara missed all four of his 3-point attempts over that span.

Even so, McNamara understands he'll always be tagged a shooter.

"In the first half, they just weren't going in," McNamara said. "They felt good leaving my hand, but they weren't falling. The coaches told me to keep shooting. Shooters shoot."

McNamara's teammates more than made up for his early inability to hit.

All five Syracuse starters finished in double figures for the first time this season. In four games against major-conference opponents, Syracuse finished with more than three players in double figures just once.

Missouri was led by point guard Ricky Clemons, who totaled 26 points. Only two other Tigers, Arthur Johnson (17 points) and Rickey Paulding (11), managed double digits.

"You have to have balance to play good basketball," Boeheim said. "We said earlier when Carmelo had 37 and nobody else had double figures that that wasn't good. He's going to have bad nights."

In Syracuse's lone loss, to Memphis, Anthony scored 27 points, but only he and McNamara scored more than 10.

The Tigers used a series of double-teams to hold Anthony, the Big East's leading scorer, to 16 points, his lowest total. Unfortunately for the Tigers, the strategy backfired, leaving SU's other scorers free.

"We knew they had a bunch of weapons," Clemons said. "They showed that tonight. We wanted to contain Anthony and double him up sometimes. We did a good job doing that. But everybody else got going."

In the first half, Warrick got going. He kept the Orangemen in the game, scoring 12 points on 6-of-10 shooting.

"Sometime in the first half, I heard their coach yelling, 'You can't leave Warrick alone anymore,' " Warrick said.

Even Syracuse's centers, who played poorly in the season's first few weeks, pitched in on offense. Craig Forth, who finished with 11 points, began the game with an open dunk after Missouri doubled Anthony.

Forth, booed often by students at the season's start, left to a standing ovation after starting the second half with a pair of layups and a baseline jumper.

"This was a statement game," Anthony said. "This was a top-15 team, and we wanted to prove that we belong in the Top 25. That's how we came out and played." ∎

SEASON PLAY BY PLAY

Warrick stages coming out party in win over Tigers

COLUMN BY ELI SASLOW

One by one, they pulled him aside. Head coach Jim Boeheim first, then assistant coaches Mike Hopkins and Troy Weaver. Next, 12 teammates wanted to talk to him. Then his mom and uncle called from back home in Philadelphia, because they had to be in on this, too.

Everyone came to talk to Hakim Warrick after the sophomore struggled in SU's Jan. 8 win over Seton Hall. Fifteen minutes, that's all everyone asked for. So Warrick gave his time even though he already knew what would be said.

Hakim, we need you. You have to play better, have to play tougher. Look for your shot. You can play with these guys. Be confident. Be aggressive.

Be quiet. That's the message Warrick delivered to the procession in SU's last two games. Saturday night against Boston College, he scored 24 and grabbed a career-high 15 rebounds. Last night against Missouri, he scored 20 and took 10 off the glass.

"I showed everybody that I can play, and I'm just fine," Warrick said after Syracuse beat Missouri, 76-69, last night. "I'm more confident right now than I have been at Syracuse. I'll look for my shot, take it and then make it."

And then trash talk in an opponent's face. Against Missouri, Warrick — who was bullied and bruised by tough teams last year — tried to intimidate.

After he blocked the shot of 270-pound Missouri center Arthur

Johnson, Warrick bumped chests with Johnson and delivered a tirade that, even without sound, probably had ESPN producers flinching.

"That's pretty unusual for Hakim," SU guard Josh Pace said. "He doesn't get angry much. But it's a big game, and he's been more aggressive lately."

Said Warrick: "In the heat of the moment, I probably said some things. I was like, 'Boy, you better get ready. I'm gonna own you all night.' "

And he did. Warrick scored most of his points off 12-foot fadeaways that had every Missouri player confused. With his back to the basket, Warrick would fake right, spin left, jump and shoot. Most of the time, he made the shot. Once, he didn't and was fouled.

Warrick — once gun-shy outside his dunking range — called for the ball and looked for his shot. Coming into last night's game, he had 33 dunks. Last night, he had none but found other ways to score.

"Hakim can make his shot," Boeheim said. "He works really hard on that. He's at the point where he can make it regularly."

The only shots Warrick didn't make were the jumpers he couldn't shoot spinning and fading away. He made just 4 of 11 free throws, again showing the Achilles' heel that's haunted him since the end of last year.

But every other part of Warrick's game seems improved from his freshman season, when he averaged six points and five rebounds. Through 12 games this year, he's averaging 17 points and nine boards.

"I give Hakim all my props," freshman Carmelo Anthony said. "He's a lot better than I thought he would be before I came here. He carried us sometimes tonight. He's been huge."

"I'm learning that you have to do a lot of things to get around people out there," Warrick said. "You've got to have a bunch of moves, know when to fake and stuff. There are a lot of big guys out there who can play."

And now Warrick has made it clear — to his procession and others — that he's one of them. ∎

Pittsburgh too physical for untested Orangemen

STORY BY CHICO HARLAN | PHOTOS BY AMY YOUNG

PITTSBURGH — Down low, one team shielded space while the other yielded space. One team pulled down rebounds as the other pulled itself out of the game with turnovers. While one team chalked up second-chance points, the other only talked about getting a second chance.

The case study in contrasts left Syracuse with a definitive answer that it's still a few shipments of grit and muscle from the Big East's top rung.

Experienced No. 2 Pittsburgh, 14-1 overall, 4-0 in the league for the first time, displayed a defensive know-how that the Orangemen couldn't match, and that was demonstrated convincingly in SU's 73-60 loss before 12,508 at the Petersen Events Center.

"Our offense just wasn't good enough today," SU head coach Jim Boeheim said, "and the majority of the reason for that is Pittsburgh is just very experienced and very, very good defensively. We hadn't faced anyone as physical as Pittsburgh is.

"If they're not the best defensive team in the country, they're pretty close to it."

Syracuse (11-2, 2-1 Big East), which entered with the fifth-best scoring offense in the country, mustered its lowest point total of the season. Meanwhile, the Panthers continued to assert themselves with a defense that's on pace to become the stingiest in Big East history.

That defense limited SU to just 45 field-goal attempts. It forced the Orangemen into a season-high 20 turnovers. It held superfrosh Carmelo Anthony to a super-pedestrian 14 points and three rebounds.

"Am I surprised we didn't win? No. Not when you have 20 turnovers. Not when you look at the stat sheet."

CRAIG FORTH
SU CENTER

"In our locker room before the game," Anthony said, "our coach said Pitt was going to play physical. So they started throwing 'bows, and I got out of sync a little bit."

So did Anthony's teammates. Syracuse couldn't find a third scoring option — let alone a primary or secondary option — in part because the rash of turnovers kept the offense from settling in.

Pesky 6-foot-4 guard Jaron Brown spent his time on defense attached to Anthony like an umbilical cord. He snagged eight rebounds and rarely let Syracuse's leading scorer beat him off the dribble.

"(Brown) was out there, playing real aggressive, real scrappy," said forward Hakim Warrick, who scored 11 points — four of which came in the final two minutes, when the game was already decided. "He's all over you the whole game. He was able to get a few rebounds nobody thought he could get."

The Panthers held a 35-27 edge on the boards, mostly because of a 15-8 discrepancy in offensive rebounding. In fact, when the Orangemen bolted away to an early 19-12 lead, offensive rebounds pumped Pittsburgh back into the game.

Senior Donatas Zavackas followed a Brown miss for a layup that put Pitt up, 24-22. One minute later, Julius Page — who finished with a career-high 25 points — poured in back-to-back 3-pointers, and the previously quieted Pitt student section rose into a bouncing throng.

The performances of Page, Zavackas and Chevon Troutman — who combined to equal the entire Syracuse offensive output — offset the lackluster outing from Brandin Knight. Pitt's star point guard was stonewalled into his first scoreless game of the season. But it didn't matter.

"We have so much depth," Pittsburgh coach Ben Howland said. "You can't say, 'If we stop Brandin, then you'll beat Pittsburgh.' To stop Pittsburgh, you have to stop a lot of guys."

Syracuse did plenty to stop itself.

The SU deficit swelled to double digits in the second half, when Troutman, who made 10 of his 12 shots, swiped the ball from Anthony and converted a gimme layup.

One timeout and two possessions later, Panther freshman Carl Krauser forced yet another turnover, swerved down the court and dished a no-look pass to Page, who finished the play with an emphatic dunk.

"I think we'll get better, but at this stage we just didn't handle the defensive effort that Pitt made," Boeheim said. "They forced us into some things that we really didn't want to do."

Converting points from turnovers, Pittsburgh had 33. Syracuse? Just 11.

"Am I surprised we didn't win?" SU center Craig Forth asked. "No. Not when you have 20 turnovers. Not when you look at the stat sheet. Not when I have one rebound. We played hard the whole game, but not well." ∎

Edelin's long-awaited debut not worth the time, hype

STORY BY DARRYL SLATER

PITTSBURGH — Billy Edelin chomped on a piece of gum, tapping his foot. He appeared nervous as he waited to enter a Syracuse men's basketball regular-season game for the first time.

Edelin, who was suspended for all of last year and 12 games this season, played seven minutes in the Orangemen's 73-60 loss to Pittsburgh on Saturday. He entered with 9:30 left in the first half and finished with two points, one rebound and a turnover.

Asked if he was as nervous as he looked on the bench, Edelin said, "I didn't really get a chance to be. Maybe if I were out there longer."

"He was really hyped, ready to get out there," SU forward Hakim Warrick said.

Edelin sat out last year after two female SU students accused him of sexual misconduct. The NCAA suspended him 12 games this season for playing in non-sanctioned recreational-league games.

On Saturday, SU head coach Jim Boeheim planned to limit Edelin's minutes.

"I didn't want this game to be put on Billy," he said.

Edelin played his natural point-guard position, and the Orangemen were called for a shot-clock violation on his first possession.

The crowd rode Edelin even harder than the Panthers' defense. One fan screamed: "You belong in jail, Bill!" Another in the student section held up a sign that read: "Yo Billy, No Means No."

KNIGHT FIRES BLANKS

Syracuse focused its defensive efforts on stopping Pitt point guard Brandin Knight.

While the Panthers got double-digit points from three players, Knight was a non-factor. He was 0-for-6 shooting, including 0 for 4 from 3-point range.

"We were fortunate that we caught him not having a good game," Boeheim said. "But I don't worry about one guy when we play Pittsburgh. You've got to worry about all the guys."

With Knight slumping, shooting guard Julius Page scorched the Orangemen for 25 points.

PRESSING MATTERS

With 11:30 left in the game, the Orangemen tried a full-court press.

The Panthers easily cracked SU's defense, and center Ontario Lett delivered an uncontested layup.

"They didn't have much trouble with it," Boeheim said. "It's a long shot, but when the clock starts getting low, you have to try long shots sometimes."

THIS AND THAT

The game was the Orangemen's first in Pitt's new Petersen Events Center. The posh facility, which sold out every game before the season, features a media room named after ESPN college football analyst Beano Cook, the school's sports information director from 1956-66. ... Former Pitt football player and NFL Hall of Famer Tony Dorsett attended the game. ... The win gave Pitt its first 4-0 conference start since the Panthers joined the Big East in 1982. ... Knight and brother Brevin, who played at Stanford, rank 34th on the all-time NCAA brother scoring combinations. For the record, Larry and Eddie Bird are fourth. ■

Orangemen defense pilfers victory from Pirates

STORY BY CHRIS CARLSON | PHOTOS BY JAMES PINSKY

Seton Hall thought it had fixed this problem already.

A paltry perimeter shooting percentage hampered the Pirates in their first game against Syracuse. Then guards Andre Barrett and John Allen seemingly regained their shooting strokes in wins over Georgetown and Miami.

But the return of Syracuse's 2-3 zone sent Barrett and Allen spiraling back to their struggles. The two combined to shoot 7 for 33 — including 5 of 14 from 3-point range — as the Syracuse men's basketball team dominated the Pirates, 83-65, in front of 17,119 at the Carrier Dome.

"It's tough to have a chance if you don't make shots," Seton Hall head coach Louis Orr said. "We have to make some perimeter shots to have a chance against the zone."

The Pirates didn't. And SU (12-2, 3-1 Big East) turned in its most complete defensive effort of the conference season.

"We did a much better job in the lane, then we got out on their shooters," Syracuse head coach Jim Boeheim said. "Our defense was much better inside."

With 7:40 left in the first half, the game was tied, 15-15. Freshman center Kelly Whitney had scored seven of Seton Hall's first 15 and buried his first three field-goal attempts.

But Whitney — who dominated Syracuse inside in the first meeting and again led Seton Hall with 23 points — managed only two more shots the rest of the half.

SU forward Hakim Warrick sagged from his position in the corner of SU's 2-3 zone. With Warrick blanketing Whitney from the front and center Jeremy McNeil shoving him out of the lane from the back, Seton Hall (7-8, 2-4) struggled to get the ball inside.

The defensive strategy catapulted Syracuse to a 19-5 run, and Seton Hall never led again. The Pirates spent the majority of their offensive sets trying to force the ball inside, and after being denied by Syracuse's interior defense, were forced to settle for contested 3-pointers.

"It felt like a lot of the time they had to shoot as the shot clock was running out," Warrick said. "We worked on our inside defense a lot after (the last SHU-SU) game. We knew that's how they got a lot of their baskets."

While Seton Hall struggled from behind the arc, Syracuse —

specifically point guard Gerry McNamara — prospered. McNamara scored eight points during the spurt, including two 3-pointers, while Warrick contributed six. Warrick (22 points) and McNamara (21 points) led five Orangemen in double figures.

In addition to helping set up SU's offense, Warrick also limited Whitney's shot attempts. Whitney — the Pirates' most dominant offensive player — was held to 11 shots. The ineffective tandem of

Barrett and Allen hoisted 33.

"Some guys had really rough nights," Orr said. "We weren't in attack mode. We weren't driving and dishing. There aren't many nights when Allen's going to shoot 1 for 15."

Seton Hall began the second half by closing the gap to seven after Barrett made a pair of 3-pointers, but Syracuse clamped down its defense again.

Boeheim's lone complaint about Syracuse's defensive effort was the ease with which Barrett moved into the lane. Barrett often found his way through the first layer of Syracuse defenders.

But fortunately for SU, he looked lost among the second wave.

Barrett shot 1 for 8 from inside the arc, forcing floaters over Syracuse's inside defenders.

Syracuse's defense converged on Barrett, as well as the teammates he found with interior passes. As Pirates went up expecting uncontested layups, they met a wall of Syracuse arms.

Carmelo Anthony and McNeil led an interior defense that collected 10 blocked shots. Anthony blocked four while McNeil sent back three, one when he pinned an attempted dunk by Whitney against the backboard.

With the Orangemen leading, 55-43, the defense put the game out of reach. A steal led to a fast-break dunk from McNeil. Then a blocked shot by Warrick allowed guard Kueth Duany to convert a baseline jumper.

Orr was forced to call a timeout, but the Orangemen continued on with a 16-7 spurt.

"We were in their face the whole game," Duany said. "We were a lot bigger than they were. We just took their shots away from them." ■

Face it: McNamara one of Big East's best players

COLUMN BY PETE IORIZZO

How dare he? It's like ripping Ghandi for being too passive. Or calling out Halle Berry for being too beautiful.

But Andre Barrett — now twice bested by Gerry McNamara, most recently in SU's 83-65 dismantling of Seton Hall at the Carrier Dome last night — dared to question the game of Scranton's Golden Boy.

"He knocks down open shots, that's what we're supposed to do," Barrett said, questioning McNamara's one-dimensionality. "I haven't seen him play point guard, really. He just hits open shots, like we're supposed to."

Down the hall, McNamara, standing as calmly as he does when executing his smooth release, held court while a mob of video cameras, microphones and tape recorders implored him to speak. Finally, when court was dismissed, McNamara stretched his back and, in his typically nonchalant way, answered a few more questions.

He decided, completely unprompted, to praise Barrett.

"Barrett's probably the best defensive player I've gone up against," McNamara said. "He was shadowing me the whole night."

Then he was made aware of Barrett's remarks.

"He said that?" McNamara gasped in disbelief. "Well if all I do is hit open shots, then where the hell was he all night?"

Clearly not close enough to cast a shadow on McNamara, who without a shadow of a doubt has established himself as one of the Big East's best point guards.

Last night, as Barrett pointed out, McNamara nailed the open shots, accounting for 21 points. But Barrett ignored McNamara's six assists and his defense, which helped limit Seton Hall's starting guards to 7-of-33 shooting, including 5 of 14 from beyond the 3-point line.

Not everyone on the Pirates' bench was as blind to the obvious as Barrett.

"(McNamara's) one of the better guards in the league," SHU head coach Louis Orr said. "He's a good offensive threat, but I'm even more impressed with the way he runs the team. He can hurt you with his shot, but he's also not going to make many mistakes."

So far McNamara's record is flawless. He's gone up against Barrett twice and outplayed him both times. He stayed with Boston College's Troy Bell, and, in defeat, outscored Pitt's Brandin Knight, 19-0.

Seems we got it backward. We heard about how McNamara had to face Barrett. Then Bell. Then Knight. Time to reverse it. Now McNamara's name comes first.

"I'm not going to say I'm one of the best point guards in the Big East," McNamara said. "But I've held my own, if not outplayed some of them."

By doing so, he's made the players around him better. As opponents worry about McNamara and fellow freshman Carmelo Anthony, things have opened up for others, like Hakim Warrick, who went 8 of 11 with 22 points and 10 rebounds last night.

Off the court, McNamara fits the star role, too. He kindly signs autographs for the flock of youngsters that migrates to his locker after games.

"When you're a kid, you want someone's autograph," McNamara said. "To play that role when you're older, it doesn't get any better than that."

And despite Barrett's objections, in terms of Big East point guards, it doesn't get any better than McNamara. ∎

Miami shoots blanks as Syracuse wins ugly game

STORY BY PETE IORIZZO | PHOTOS BY NATALIA JIMENEZ

CORAL GABLES, Fla. — Perry Clark's two daughters should be thankful the Miami head coach resisted the urge to make a wager.

"I would've bet my family," he said, "we wouldn't get shut out the last eight minutes."

Such a bet would've left the Clark clan stranded. His punchless Hurricanes indeed failed to score during the last 8:38 of the game, allowing the Syracuse men's basketball team to escape Miami yesterday with a 54-49 win in front of 5,789 at the Convocation Center.

Syracuse won despite poor shooting from freshmen Gerry McNamara and Carmelo Anthony. In fact, SU (13-2, 4-1 Big East) barely outdid Miami's (8-8, 1-4) futility during the infamous eight-minute span, converting only one field goal.

But the Orangemen's defense, as it did last Wednesday against Seton Hall, held.

"At the end of the game, we knew (Darius) Rice and (James) Jones were going to take the shots," SU head coach Jim Boeheim said. "I saw Rice put up 43 against Connecticut on Monday night. We weren't going to let them get open looks."

Even when they did, Rice and Jones mostly misfired. They combined for 9-of-29 shooting and 24 points. Before yesterday, they had combined to average 37.

Rice and Jones' paltry shooting became most apparent during the Hurricanes' eight-minute drought, when the two forwards shot a combined 0 of 8.

With 8:38 left, Jones spun near the lane and knocked down a jumper to put Miami ahead, 49-45. The Hurricanes followed that, though, by missing 3-pointers on four of their next seven possessions.

By the time Rice missed the fourth 3-pointer, Syracuse had taken a 50-49 lead on a Hakim Warrick dunk, Syracuse's only field goal during the last eight minutes.

"We had the right guys taking the shots," Clark said. "We just couldn't make anything. The zone makes you make basketball plays. We did that in the first half. In the second, we did not."

In the first half, Miami seemed to take control, finishing with a 17-5 run. Anthony sunk a 3-pointer to give Syracuse a 20-13 lead with 8:05 left in the half, but the Orangemen converted only one field goal the rest of the half — a 3-pointer from McNamara.

The first 20 minutes ended with the Hurricanes up, 30-25, but they managed only 19 second-half points.

"I thought we played real good defensively through the whole course of the game," Anthony said. "We did a good job on Rice and James. We knew where they were all the time. (In the last eight minutes), we came out and challenged them a little more than what we'd been doing."

For as well as Syracuse executed its 2-3 zone, the Hurricanes managed to stay in the game because McNamara and Anthony combined for 5-of-25 shooting and 15 points. Before yesterday, they had averaged 37.7 combined.

While Anthony has suffered through a few off nights, McNamara has been the model of consistency. Before yesterday's three-point, 1-for-10-shooting performance, he had yet to score below 17 in a conference game.

During the last 32:05 of the game, neither Anthony nor McNamara hit a shot. Anthony got his three second-half points off free throws.

"It's just one of those days," McNamara said. "I'll be back."

The Orangemen might have lost — despite Miami's 31.7-shooting percentage — if not for the efforts of Kueth Duany and Warrick.

Duany, who this season has been as inconsistent as McNamara has been consistent, finished with 17 points, his most in five games. After a subpar, four-point first half, Warrick responded with 14 in the second.

"We're a team," Duany said. "Carmelo and Gerry have carried us through some of the games. But it's a win, and that's the most important thing." ■

Energetic Warrick again ignites Syracuse with dunks

BY PETE IORIZZO AND DARRYL SLATER | PHOTOS BY NATALIA JIMENEZ

CORAL GABLES, Fla. — Eyes wide and a snarl curling up on his lips, Hakim Warrick stared down Miami forward Gary Hamilton and screamed excitedly, "Woo! Let's go!"

Warrick had just slam-dunked a Kueth Duany missed 3-pointer to give the Syracuse men's basketball team a one-point lead. He was guarding Hamilton, who was inbounding the ball.

While the Orangemen pulled away down the stretch, Hamilton and the Hurricanes failed to heed Warrick's advice. They faded in a 54-49 SU win yesterday afternoon.

Warrick's dunk, with 5:58 left in the game, put Syracuse up, 50-49, and gave SU a lead it never relinquished. Warrick had a game-high 18 points, 14 in the second half. His dunk was the last SU field goal of the game. In the final 9:47, Warrick scored the Orangemen's only two field goals.

"He brought a lot of energy," Miami head coach Perry Clark said. "In the second half, he was more aggressive in his play than we were in trying to stop him."

Warrick shot just 1 of 4 in the first half, and SU head coach Jim Boeheim was quick to admonish the sophomore.

"I got on him big in the first half," Boeheim said. "I told him the reason he was open from 20 feet is because he can't shoot from there. It's a good reason when you're open. Players sometimes don't understand that.

"Guys come over to the bench and say they're open, and I say, 'Yeah, for a good reason, because you can't make that shot.' In the second half,

TURNING POINT >>

With 5:58 left in the game, Hakim Warrick slammed home Kueth Duany's missed 3-pointer to give SU a 50-49 lead. Warrick's dunk was the only SU field goal — and the game's only field goal — in the final 8:38.

BOX SCORE

(8-8, I-4)

HURRICANES	P	R	A
Rice	13	11	2
James	11	5	2
Hite	10	6	0
Simmons	8	1	4
Berumen	5	2	0
Surratt	2	5	3
Hamilton	0	0	5
Wilkins	0	1	0
Coelho	0	0	0
Djahue	0	2	0

	I	2	F
SYRACUSE	25	29	**54**
MIAMI	30	19	**49**

(13-2, 4-I)

ORANGEMEN	P	R	A
Warrick	18	5	0
Duany	17	4	4
Anthony	12	14	1
Forth	4	4	0
McNamara	3	3	4
McNeil	0	2	0
Edelin	0	1	3

SEASON PLAY BY PLAY

he got in the middle, and that's where he can do things."

Playing primarily as the Orangemen's third scoring option, Warrick has scored at least 18 points in four of SU's last five games.

"He's been coming up pretty good for us," Boeheim said.

OFF PACE

Josh Pace has always felt comfortable coming off the bench. But these days, he's getting more time to get comfortable on the bench.

Against Miami yesterday, Pace never shed his warm-ups, recording his first DNP of the season.

"(The Hurricanes) made up their minds that they were going to play a zone," Boeheim said. "I wasn't going to put a non-shooter in there."

Lately, Pace hasn't even had a chance to shoot. Since playing 26 minutes against Boston College on Jan. 11, his minutes have dwindled: 18 against Missouri, 10 at Pittsburgh and three versus Seton Hall. Pace has not scored in the last three games.

Pace's minutes have been most affected by the return of Billy Edelin, who's averaged 16 minutes of action since returning from a 12-game, NCAA-imposed suspension against Pittsburgh.

Yesterday, Edelin played 14 minutes — nine in the first half and five in the second — and missed his only shot. He dished three assists but turned the ball over three times.

"Billy played like he did against Pittsburgh," Boeheim said. "I went with him early, because I thought he'd play well. He hasn't played in one-and-a-half years. I'm going strictly on a guessing game. I have no idea what he's going to do."

THIS AND THAT

The loss was Miami's first in the Convocation Center, which opened Jan. 4. The Hurricanes are now 2-1 in their new digs. ... Miami hasn't defeated Syracuse here since 1996. ... Though he struggled late, Miami forward Darius Rice had his first double-double of the season (13 points, 11 rebounds). ... The Syracuse women's basketball team, winners over Miami on Saturday night, attended yesterday's game before catching a flight home. ... On Friday, daytime temperatures dipped into the 50s in the Miami area. A four-minute local news segment titled "South Florida Shivers" included a graphic in the lower right-hand corner of the screen with the temperature (57 degrees) and the words "Big Chill." Tough life.∎

Syracuse win? Don't bank on it against Rutgers

STORY BY CHRIS CARLSON | PHOTOS BY AMY YOUNG

PISCATAWAY, N.J. — It didn't take much for Rutgers to earn its first Big East win. Just the ability to survive a 21-6 run, another stellar game in a string of spectacular outings by guard Jerome Coleman and a miracle 3-point bank shot.

That's all.

The Syracuse men's basketball team's 68-65 loss to Rutgers last night in front of a sellout crowd of 8,007 at the Louis Brown Athletic Center had more twists than the most complex maze. Herve Lamizana provided the final dagger, banking in a 3-point shot with 17 seconds left and the shot clock winding down.

"You could see they were heartbroken," Coleman said. "You could see they weren't coming back."

The Orangemen might wish they had never made their comeback to set up Lamizana's heave.

"Sometimes people will tell you they'd rather lose by 10 points than lose like we did," SU freshman Gerry McNamara said.

On the possession after Lamizana's shot, SU freshman Carmelo Anthony dribbled the ball toward the right wing and tried to match Lamizana's off-balance prayer with one of his own. Anthony's, though, hit the front of the rim, allowing Rutgers to run out the clock.

Still, the fact that the Orangemen were in that position at all was a minor miracle.

Midway through the second half, the Scarlet Knights led Syracuse

SEASON PLAY BY PLAY

47-35 after Jerome Coleman buried three consecutive 3-pointers, forcing Syracuse head coach Jim Boeheim to use a timeout.

First, Coleman fired over McNamara's head from outside the top of the key. Then, he moved over to the right wing and swished another. On the third, he took a step back, shot, and hopped down the court, shaking his right hand like it was burning.

In the process, Coleman singed Syracuse for nine of his game-high 31 points. He was aided by Lamizana (11 points, 14 rebounds) and Ricky Shields (14 points).

"When (Coleman) feels it, I don't care where or when he's at," Rutgers coach Gary Waters said. "He got hot. For some reason, they were playing a couple feet off him. He'd pass, get the ball back and be surprised he could shoot."

Coleman's performance against the SU zone defense shouldn't have surprised the Orangemen. Coleman scored 27 against SU last year — including seven 3-pointers — during the Orangemen's Feb. 2 loss at Rutgers.

After a poor start to his season, during which he was sapped of energy and strength by a flu-like illness (he lost 12 pounds), Coleman has scored 30 points in two consecutive games.

After Coleman's run, Syracuse, which turned the ball over 17 times to the Scarlet Knights' full-court press defense, turned to some pressure of its own.

The Scarlet Knights rushed shots, allowing Anthony and SU center Jeremy McNeil to score easy baskets in transition. After Rutgers eventually maneuvered through Syracuse's full-court press, McNeil stuffed the Scarlet Knights at the rim.

While protecting SU's basket, McNeil collected seven blocks, helping the Orangemen on their 21-6 run.

The anemic Syracuse offense, considered the team's strength at the start of the year, accumulated a horrid assist-to-turnover ratio, turning the ball over 17 times to eight assists, while making only 1 of 9 from 3-point range.

McNamara (12 points) and Anthony (17 points) were the only SU starters who scored in double-figures. The normally reliable Hakim Warrick was bullied by RU's Sean Axani and managed just six points.

Thanks to their defensive presence, the Orangemen managed a 56-53 lead before the Scarlet Knights got hot again. Each team traded runs until the end of the game.

"We were out of it and made a great comeback," Boeheim said. "We had no business being in this game."

The second half back-and-forth battle erased memories of a putrid first half, in which both teams had more turnovers than assists. Syracuse had 12 giveaways, but Rutgers kept the score tied, 27-27, at halftime by shooting 10-for-38 from the field, including 2 of 11 on three-point attempts.

All of which set the stage for Lamizana's heroics.

"I was too open for it not to go in," Lamizana said. "I was confident, almost cocky. I knew it was going in."

If he did, he was the only one.

"That's a shot we give to him," Boeheim said. "He misses that 99 out of 100 times. They had a lucky shot to beat us. I doubt anyone in that locker room will tell you that's a skilled shot." ■

For a change, Boeheim actually praises McNeil

COLUMN BY ELI SASLOW

PISCATAWAY, N.J. — Jeremy McNeil is used to taking the blame for losses like these. After Syracuse falls, head coach Jim Boeheim often points to McNeil first. Sometimes, the center was too inactive on offense, other times too slow on defense.

Once last year, Boeheim even said: "It's tough, because with Jeremy out there, it's like we're playing four-on-five on offense."

McNeil's spent the better part of four years taking up residence in Boeheim's doghouse. So when the SU center got his first peek outside after last night's 68-65 loss to Rutgers, it felt pretty good.

"Usually, I'm the one who blows (the game)," McNeil said. "But Coach actually thought I did real good tonight. I can't really remember the last time that happened."

In fact, Boeheim credited McNeil with keeping Syracuse in the game. The junior scored 10 points on 5-of-5 shooting, grabbed seven rebounds and blocked seven shots in 24 minutes.

When Syracuse went to a full-court press late, McNeil guarded the basket flawlessly. He swatted away four would-be layups in the last 12 minutes, allowing Syracuse to make a 12-point comeback and briefly take the lead.

"Jeremy was simply tremendous in the back of the defense," Boeheim said. "He single-handedly kept us in it. He played a fantastic game. Really, tremendous defensively."

His offense wasn't bad, either. Rutgers chose to double-team

Syracuse freshman Carmelo Anthony, which often left McNeil open under the basket. Five times, McNeil had easy opportunities within three feet of the rim, and he converted them all.

Still, it seemed the highlight of McNeil's night came after the game and in the locker room. When told of Boeheim's public praise and given a stat sheet, McNeil's eyes nearly popped out of his head.

"Damn, I was real good this game," he said. "This is the best game I've had since I've been at Syracuse. If we had won, this would be my best moment. That's the only thing that didn't go right for me."

Actually, one other thing went wrong, too, and it left McNeil wearing a large wrap on his right wrist after the game. After one of his late blocks, McNeil rocked his hand on the rim and came down holding his right arm. He left the game for two minutes but re-entered.

"It's not serious," McNeil said. "I know it will be fine. I'll be back right away, and I'll be more confident than ever. I needed this game. I needed something like this to get me going. I wasn't playing good before, I wasn't doing nothing. Now, I feel like I'm ready to knock some people."

"He played great," said center Craig Forth, who had eight points and five boards. "Confidence is huge for him. He'll get going high now, and that will carry him. Sometimes, he just gets a little bit down on himself."

Three-plus years in the doghouse can do that to you. It can also tempt you to transfer, which McNeil nearly did last year.

Early last season, he left the team for a few days and went home to Texas to seek counsel from his family. A few days later, he begged his way back onto the team.

"I've never been happier to be here," McNeil said last night. "My game's feeling good, and we've got a real good team. You have a game like this, and it can turn stuff around. This is what I needed. Now I'm going to keep playing like this." ■

Orangemen shock No. 2 Pitt in Dome classic

STORY BY DARRYL SLATER | PHOTOS BY ZACK SECKLER

In so many ways, the game defied convention.

Three court rushes? A successful Syracuse man-to-man defense? The soft touch of Jeremy McNeil?

As surprise one-upped surprise and shocker trumped shocker, the Syracuse men's basketball team pulled off its most exhilarating victory in three years.

The No. 24 Orangemen, some sweat-soaked and shirtless, skipped off the Carrier Dome floor Saturday night having upset No. 2 Pittsburgh, 67-65, before a crowd of 30,303, the largest to watch a college basketball game on any campus this season.

In replicating the excitement of their January 2000 upset of Connecticut, the Orangemen (14-3, 5-2 Big East) pulled off the near-impossible.

They trimmed a 14-point second-half deficit. Survived — flourished even — playing man-to-man defense. Waded three times through paint-clad fans, many of whom hopped on players' backs, perhaps hoping to be carried to the SU locker room, where a more subdued celebration, set to rap music, ensued.

"I haven't ever seen anything like this," guard Josh Pace said.

"I was body surfing with some guys," fifth-year senior Kueth Duany said.

Down 12 at halftime, the Orangemen whittled Pittsburgh's (15-2, 5-1) lead before McNeil went to the free-throw line with 46.9 seconds left.

"I was scared to death," he said.

Several Orangemen sitting on the bench turned to each other.

"You think he'll make it?" they asked.

"He doesn't make them in *practice*," SU head coach Jim Boeheim said afterward.

McNeil sunk both free throws to tie the game, 65-65.

After Pitt inbounded the ball, Carmelo Anthony stole it from Jaron Brown and called timeout with 10.4 seconds left.

Boeheim called a clear-out play for freshman Gerry McNamara, who sliced to the basket and tossed up an off-balance layup. Pitt center Ontario Lett cut across the paint to defend McNamara, leaving McNeil wide open to tap in McNamara's miss with three seconds left, giving SU a 67-65 lead.

"The ball just happened to bounce to my side," McNeil said.

Pitt's Brandin Knight inbounded the ball to Carl Krauser, who fumbled the pass while trying to call timeout. Thinking the game was over, students rushed the court. But officials checked the television replay and determined that Krauser's timeout call was acknowledged with 0.8 seconds left. SU players and police corralled fans off the court.

After Pitt's timeout, Brown tossed an inbound pass to Knight, who was just past halfcourt. Knight bobbled the pass and then swished a 3-pointer. Again, fans swarmed the floor, thinking Knight's shot was too late. As officials checked the replay, Boeheim grabbed a microphone and screamed for fans to leave the floor. With some fans still milling about the court, referee Ed Corbett ruled Knight's shots went in after the buzzer.

The celebration commenced, as SU's Anthony and Pace hopped on the scorer's table and tore off their jerseys. Anthony twirled his over his head.

Fans nearly pinned SU associate head coach Bernie Fine against the scorer's table.

"It's a good thing I'm a decent-sized guy," Fine said, "because it was getting kind of tight."

While the celebration raged on, McNeil, the game's hero, escaped to the bowels of the Carrier Dome, where he quietly lifted weights with strength coach Todd Forcier.

Dripping with sweat, McNeil was the last Orangeman to emerge for postgame interviews.

"Shoot, we're just thirsty," McNeil said. "We were just dogs today. We were playing good defense, and it all paid off."

Indeed, SU abandoned its 2-3 zone defense for a man-to-man set with three minutes left in the first half and held the Panthers scoreless for 5:30 in the second half.

"Without any doubt, (it is) the best defense we've played in a long time," Boeheim said. "Realistically, I didn't think we'd be able to play them man-to-man. Our defense is what won the game."

That and the efforts of Duany and Hakim Warrick. Duany scored 15 points, and Warrick had 20, 14 of which came in the second half.

The Orangemen held Knight, playing with a sprained left ankle, to 3-of-12 shooting, including 0 of 8 from 3-point range.

"It would've been heartbreaking if we had lost," Boeheim said. "But we weren't going to let it go." ■

Boeheim shows Pitt game is no normal victory

COLUMN BY PETE IORIZZO

If the final score and three court rushings and 30,303 hysterical fans and Josh Pace dancing shirtless on the scorer's table — a subsequently *broken* scorer's table — and Kueth Duany body surfing and Craig Forth tossing to and fro in a sea of orange and Gerry McNamara barreling through an overzealous crowd didn't say this was a big win, Jim Boeheim did.

The Syracuse men's basketball coach said it without a long, eloquent waxing or even a few short, memorable lines. Instead, that extra zing in his usually monotonous voice in his postgame press conference said it. So did his ruffled hair, normally so perfect. Ditto for the abundance of comical one-liners.

But most of all, Boeheim said it with what he didn't say in the locker room afterward.

"I don't think he yelled at us," Forth said. "He does pretty much every time. Not this time."

He could have, too. It would have been all-too typical of Boeheim to begin his media address by acknowledging a nice comeback, only to digress into a string of "We're not where we need to be yet," "Our defense needs work" and the customary "Kueth didn't have it tonight."

Instead, Boeheim almost immediately praised Duany — "Kueth Duany was all over the court today on defense, helping people and making plays" — and then SU's man-to-man defense.

When he went out of his way to praise even the fans, there was no denying it. The Syracuse coach of 27 years and 637 victories was pumped.

When Boeheim finished his opening remarks, he paused to collect his breath and ran his hand through his out-of-place and receding hair, perhaps disheveled in the postgame celebration.

He must have been exhausted by that point. He'd already hollered at referee Ed Corbett during an SU timeout with 2:03 remaining in the game.

Of course, it's nothing new to see Boeheim marching along the sideline and spewing his opinions into an official's tired ear. It's equally common to see him walk over to an official at a timeout to further the discussion.

But this being a big game, Boeheim gave Corbett a larger-than-normal piece of his mind. He shouted loudly enough to be heard across the court and had to be pushed back into the huddle by freshman Carmelo Anthony.

"Coach is one of the most exciting guys on the sidelines," said former Syracuse guard Allen Griffin, who played for Boeheim from 1997 to 2001. "His demeanor might not show it, but the way he talks to the refs, you can see it."

At the, well, second end of the game, after Pitt guard Brandin Knight buried a 3-pointer a heartbeat after the final buzzer sounded, Boeheim moved into action again. He grabbed the microphone and ordered, in a loud, screeching voice, the fans to get the hell off the court.

"Calm down," he commanded. "Get off the court! Let us figure out what happened here."

So perhaps it's no surprise that toward the end of his press conference, the zip in Boeheim's voice waned. He started taking long pauses.

And he changed topics, too. He noted those missed second-half layups. He bemoaned Syracuse's poor shooting in the Big East.

And he declared that a new game, another big one too, tips off tonight. ■

Hoyas center runs wild, but Orangemen pull out with win

STORY BY CHRIS CARLSON | PHOTOS BY SETH SIDITSKY

Mike Sweetney and Craig Forth stood speechless in their respective locker rooms.

Forth had been awed into silence by Sweetney's annihilation of the No. 19 Syracuse men's basketball team's interior defense. Sweetney, meanwhile, was shushed by Syracuse's 88-80 victory in front of 20,702 at the Carrier Dome last night.

Unfortunately for Sweetney, his game-highs of 32 points, 13 rebounds and seven blocks weren't enough for the Hoyas (10-8, 2-6 Big East).

"I scored some," a sullen Sweetney said. "But they made their free throws. I didn't, and it cost us."

Despite Sweetney's assessment — he shot 10 of 19 from the free-throw line — he wowed five NBA scouts on press row who whispered to each other after nearly every basket he scored. Sweetney created space with his broad, 6-foot-8, 260-pound body, hitting layups and converting on a number of turnaround jump shots.

"I don't really know what to say," Forth said, when asked about Sweetney's play. "He's a big guy."

Syracuse forward Carmelo Anthony, though, was more than able to help the tongue-tied Forth.

"We couldn't do anything about him," Anthony said. "We tried a lot of things, and we failed in every possible way. (Strong) doesn't even begin to describe him. He dominated the whole game."

Well, not the whole game.

IN CASE YOU MISSED IT...

Syracuse is now 13-0 at home. The Orangemen score 87.2 points per game in the Carrier Dome and allow 68. On the road, SU averages 62.4 points and allows 65.2. Syracuse started the 1999-00 season 13-0 at home before losing its 14th home game, to Seton Hall.

For a span of eight minutes in the second half, Syracuse's defense restrained Georgetown's near-unstoppable force.

At the 11:08 mark, Sweetney planted himself in the lane and snatched an entry pass. As he turned to face the basket, SU guard Kueth Duany fouled him. Sweetney made 1 of 2 free throws, cutting the SU lead to 59-57.

But over the next eight minutes, the Orangemen (15-3, 6-2) held Sweetney to two points. During that span, they increased their lead to 13.

Sweetney has always dominated his counterpart, Hakim Warrick. In two meetings last year, Warrick, Syracuse's lone inside scoring threat, scored a total of nine points.

In the first half last night, Warrick continued the trend, mustering only two shots. Sweetney used his unnaturally quick feet and wide body to block Warrick's drives to the basket. When Warrick tried to spin, he spun into Sweetney. When he tried to fade away, Sweetney faded with him.

"In the first half, they were pushing and bumping (Warrick)," Anthony said. "That seemed to throw him off his rhythm."

But when Sweetney lost his scoring touch in the second half, Warrick found his. And fortunately for Warrick, Sweetney was no longer guarding him.

After scoring a layup at the 9:56 mark, Warrick caught a pass at the free-throw line, faded away, scored and was smacked on the wrist by Hoyas forward Victor Samnick.

Two possessions later, Warrick spun into the lane and was fouled by guard Brandon Bowman as he banked in a layup. Warrick shimmied his way to the free-throw line, completing a personal eight-point run and extending SU's lead to 69-59.

"(Warrick) made a couple big plays for us," SU head coach Jim Boeheim said. "Those two plays he made for us at the end were big."

After Warrick's three-point plays, Georgetown would get no closer than six points. Warrick (11 points) was helped by four other Orangemen who scored in double figures. Gerry McNamara and Anthony had 22 points each.

Still, no one came close to matching Sweetney.

"I don't think the whole Dome could have stopped him," Syracuse guard Billy Edelin said.

Maybe not. But Sweetney's teammates helped slow the big man.

The Orangemen survived Sweetney by sagging their guards in from the 3-point line. With McNamara, Edelin and Duany flashing their arms in front of Sweetney and SU's centers pressing him from behind, Sweetney's teammates struggled to pass him the ball.

When guards Tony Bethel and Bowman found their interior passing lanes cut off, they opted for outside shots. Together, Georgetown's guards shot 7 for 22, including 2 for 7 from 3-point range.

"We fronted (Sweetney) really well (during the eight-minute, second-half stretch) and forced someone else to make shots," Warrick said. "They didn't hit anything from the outside." ∎

Lights out: Torrid SU leaves West Virginia in the dark

STORY BY PETE IORIZZO | PHOTOS BY JAMES PINSKY

MORGANTOWN, W.Va. — The first two extended the lead, providing Syracuse with an eight-point, second-half comfort zone. The third put the game away, pushing SU's advantage to 13 with five minutes left.

And the fourth time Gerry McNamara lobbed an alley-oop — this one into the hands of a soaring Carmelo Anthony — it dotted the exclamation point on a 94-80 Syracuse men's basketball win Saturday over West Virginia in front of 13,092 at the West Virginia Coliseum.

By the time Anthony converted SU's fourth alley-oop, everyone had forgotten that midway through the first half, No. 19 Syracuse (16-3, 7-2 Big East) trailed by as many as 15. But by shooting 58 percent and having five players score in double figures, the Orangemen pulled off a 29-point turnaround.

"We're not going to come and shoot like this all the time," SU forward Hakim Warrick said. "But today, our shooting carried us most of the way."

Warrick finished with 18 points on 9-of-14 shooting. Anthony, the Orangemen's other starting forward, had a game-high 29 and shot 12 of 17.

Both benefited from a 1-3-1 West Virginia defense that crumbled. Syracuse's 59 percent first-half shooting, including 4 of 12 from 3-point range, prevented the Mountaineers from collapsing on Anthony and Warrick.

"That leaves some easy shots," SU guard Kueth Duany said. "They're more vulnerable, and you can just attack them deep."

Anthony, free of a double-team, struck most, recording his highest Big East point total. He and Warrick each converted two alley-oops from McNamara, who finished with a season-high 12 assists.

SEASON PLAY BY PLAY

"I just put it up toward the backboard for Hakim and at the top of the backboard for Carmelo," McNamara said. "It's fun to watch. We're fortunate to have such athletic guys who can get up there and slam it down."

McNamara mostly played shooting guard, because point guard Billy Edelin played a reliable 38 minutes. He scored a season-high 18 points and hit his first six shots before finishing 8 of 11.

The freshman point guard also helped spread the ball to the Orangemen's two forwards, collecting three assists. In the first half, he drove to the basket through open lanes, sometimes finishing with a layup and other times dishing to Warrick for easy dunks.

"He's going to find the open guy," McNamara said. "That's why I love playing with him. He creates for other people. He makes other people better."

"He's back," SU head coach Jim Boeheim said. "It's a good game for him to be in. He got a lot of good looks. He finishes as well as anyone we've had going to the basket since Sherman Douglas. When he gets in the lane, he makes that shot. It isn't always pretty, but the ball ends up where it's supposed to end up."

Edelin quarterbacked an often small Syracuse lineup. SU centers played just 14 combined minutes — starter Craig Forth played a season-low three — as Syracuse moved Duany to small forward with Edelin and McNamara as the backcourt.

But a big lineup that included Jeremy McNeil at center helped Syracuse overcome a 31-16 deficit with 11:33 remaining in the first half. Thanks in part to McNeil guarding the paint when Syracuse pressed, the Orangemen shut down the Mountaineers (12-8, 3-5) and outscored WVU, 30-16, the rest of the half.

After an 8-1 SU run started the second half, the Mountaineers never recovered. West Virginia shot only 37 percent in the second half compared to 47 percent in the first 20 minutes.

Sophomore Drew Schifino led West Virginia with 25 points and freshman Kevin Pittsnogle added 24. But their combined 19-of-40 shooting failed to overcome five Orangemen — Anthony, Warrick, Duany, McNamara and Edelin — in double figures.

Seven times this season, Syracuse has had five players hit the double-digit mark, and each time, the Orangemen have won.

"With the great teams, we've had that," Boeheim said. "In college basketball, the more balanced you are, the better chance you have. The question becomes: Who do you stop?" ■

"They were killing our zone. They were eating our zone up. The only way we were gonna stop them was to be aggressive."

KUETH DUANY
SU FORWARD ON THE
ORANGEMEN SWITCHING TO
MAN-TO-MAN DEFENSE

Man-to-man 'D' comes to the rescue again

STORY BY DARRYL SLATER

MORGANTOWN, W.Va. — For five minutes, Jim Boeheim stood on the sideline and fumed as his team stood on the court and fizzled, its defense collapsing beneath West Virginia's offensive avalanche.

The Mountaineers scored 21 points in the opening five minutes Saturday, building a nine-point lead that left Boeheim scrambling to scrap his Syracuse men's basketball team's 2-3 zone for a man-to-man defense. Though the No. 19 Orangemen struggled with man-to-man early, they settled down and eventually went back to zone in their 94-80 win over the Mountaineers.

"They were killing our zone," SU forward Kueth Duany said. "They were eating our zone up. The only way we were gonna stop them was to be aggressive."

At first, the Orangemen looked lost playing man-to-man. WVU's Kevin Pittsnogle hit two 3-pointers, the second of which SU center Jeremy McNeil made little effort to defend. On the next West Virginia possession, Drew Schifino blew by SU point guard Gerry McNamara for a layup. McNamara fouled Schifino, and Schifino's free throw gave the Mountaineers a 27-14 lead.

West Virginia stretched its lead to as many as 15, as Boeheim rubbed his head like a magic lamp, perhaps wishing for a solution to SU's defensive woes.

"When we first went to (man), we were horrendous, absolutely horrendous," Boeheim said.

But the Orangemen mounted a comeback, taking their first lead, 37-36, with 6:30 left in the first half.

"When we got back in it with our run," Boeheim said, "we did a better job with the man-to-man."

Relying mostly on man-to-man, SU allowed 16 points in the last 11:33 of the half. The Mountaineers' layups stopped falling, and Pittsnogle, at last challenged by SU defenders, went scoreless over the last 14:50 of the half.

"Once we settled down, in our zone and our man, we were all right," McNamara said.

The Orangemen started the second half in man-to-man but quickly switched to zone. After giving up 47 first-half points, tied for the most this season, they surrendered 33 in the second half.

"We got a little tired and went back to the zone," Boeheim said. "We were more effective in it the second time around. We got to the shooters better."

Boeheim said Thursday he mostly decides when to play man-to-man, which the Orangemen used to clamp down Pittsburgh in a 67-65 upset Feb. 1, during games. Often, game film fails to reveal which defense will work, Boeheim said, before adding, "You don't win or lose a game because you do or don't switch defenses."

So it seemed fitting Saturday that while the Orangemen gave up the most points they have all season — tied with last Monday's win over Georgetown — they put on their most prolific offensive showing since clobbering Albany on Dec. 28.

"All our defenses worked a little bit," Boeheim said. "But they also were all bad at times, too." ■

Backcourt struggles as SU falls to Connecticut

STORY BY CHRIS CARLSON | PHOTOS AMY YOUNG

HARTFORD, Conn. — Lately, Billy Edelin and Gerry McNamara have been the Syracuse men's basketball team's spark plugs. Last night against Connecticut, the pair was a dead engine.

Both Syracuse guards played perhaps their worst games of the season, stifling the SU offense as the No. 17 Orangemen fell, 75-61, to No. 23 UConn before 16,294 at the Hartford Civic Center.

First, McNamara struggled shooting, missing two 3-pointers on SU's first two possessions. So SU head coach Jim Boeheim brought in Edelin and hoped the freshman pairing would give the Orangemen (16-4, 7-3 Big East) offensive penetration.

McNamara shot 1 of 9, including 1 of 7 from 3-point range.

"I missed shots," McNamara said. "It just didn't go down tonight."

Edelin wasn't much better, hitting just 2 of 6 shots and turning the ball over four times.

On one of his first touches, Edelin drove the lane but misfired a pass into the hands of UConn forward Shamon Tooles. The next time Edelin touched the ball, he charged through the lane and lost the ball to Huskies center Emeka Okafor. That play brought Boeheim off the bench to scream at Edelin.

"(Edelin) was the one I was really surprised at," Boeheim said. "He looked like he had no idea what was going on today. He looked completely lost. He was like a deer in headlights."

Syracuse's guard play brought Boeheim off the bench on other occasions, too. At the end of the first half, Edelin let the clock expire, casually dribbling the ball outside the 3-point arc.

Until the 3:07 mark of the first half, only three Orangemen had scored. And forward Hakim Warrick — one of the three — scored his lone basket four minutes into the game.

"I thought (our) two guards — Ben Gordon and Tony Robertson — played terrific defense," Connecticut interim head coach George Blaney said. "Tony holding McNamara to three and Ben holding Kueth Duany to 4 for 13. I thought that was as much of a key as anything."

Still, the Orangemen managed to keep the score 30-27 by halftime, thanks to 12 points from forward Carmelo Anthony and eight from Duany.

"We got nothing offensively but (Anthony)," Boeheim said. "We can't live with just one guy. The way we played offensively we were lucky to even be in this game. (Anthony) had 29. I don't think he was the problem."

It was the rest of the Orangemen.

Syracuse's centers failed to contribute. This allowed Okafor to help UConn's guards whenever the quicker Syracuse guards tried to penetrate. Okafor was consistently several steps away from the SU centers, but Craig Forth and Jeremy McNeil still failed to score.

With no one else contributing, Anthony took the Syracuse offense on his shoulders.

At the 8:07 mark of the second half, UConn (15-5, 6-3) held a 53-49 lead after McNamara hit his only 3-pointer of the game. Over the next six possessions, Anthony fired five of Syracuse's six shots. His teammates, meanwhile, added two turnovers and two free throws.

While Anthony forced fall-away jumpers, Connecticut scored with ease. Six different Huskies scored during a 12-4 second-half run that gave UConn a 65-53 lead.

"We were terrible," Edelin said. "Guys we depend on to make plays didn't. The biggest thing we have to do is accept the fact that we didn't step up our play." ■

Huskies' balance too much for one-dimensional SU

STORY BY CHICO HARLAN

HARTFORD, Conn. — Two nifty tip-ins from two freshman no-names on two straight possessions — with that quick spurt late in the second half, the No. 23 Connecticut men's basketball team demonstrated what it had and what No. 17 Syracuse lacked.

While the SU offense teetered on the efforts of one player, forward Carmelo Anthony, the Huskies were continuously able to find third and fourth options. And sometimes, fifth and sixth options.

To finish off last night's 75-61 UConn win, a pair of those options, rookie forwards Hilton Armstrong and Marcus White, tapped in two game-icing buckets.

First, with 2:50 remaining in the game, White deflected an Emeka Okafor turnaround to extend the Husky lead to double digits.

Next time down the court, Armstrong knocked in a Ben Gordon 3-point attempt before it fell beneath the rim. Fittingly, even when Gordon and Okafor — UConn's two leading scorers — were missing shots, the Huskies never seemed to run out of options.

"We just wanted to make sure Syracuse had to worry about everyone on the court," Armstrong said.

Seven Connecticut players scored between seven and 15 points. White, the second-leading rebounder last night, and fellow freshman Rashad Anderson, the team's second-leading scorer, came off the bench.

Syracuse didn't enjoy such a luxury. The UConn bench

outscored SU's, 23-5.

"We just have more players," guard Tony Robertson said. "They only have six or seven guys, but we go nine or 10 deep. And the important thing is, all of our guys can score. Syracuse has guys inside who don't even try to score, so that kind of hurts them."

White was one of four freshmen to see significant playing time for Connecticut last night, but he displayed a veteran's knack for finding space and grabbing rebounds — often reaching over SU centers Craig Forth and Jeremy McNeil.

Playing a raw and rough style that interim head coach George Blaney describes as "street ball," White grabbed eight rebounds. Four of those came offensively.

"Man, Marcus was huge for us tonight," junior Shamon Tooles said. "We call him The Worm now, like Dennis Rodman, because he gets all the loose balls. That's his new nickname."

But it wasn't just forwards like White and Armstrong who joined UConn's raft of offensive and defensive options. As the Huskies sprinted out to a 16-4 lead, Anderson, a 6-foot-5 guard, knocked down two consecutive 3-pointers.

Bobbing back down the court with excitement, he screamed: "It's my time." And it was. In fact, it was time for every freshman on the Connecticut roster. Yesterday, the quartet of first-year players scored 38 points — better than the combined effort from SU's more heralded freshmen, despite 29 from Anthony.

The Huskies played without regular starter Taliek Brown, who sat out with a broken left finger. Because of Brown's absence, every role player in the Connecticut rotation moved into a more primary role.

"This shows we're a deep team," said Gordon, who scored 11 points, about 10 fewer than his average. "I only scored (11) points and we still come out on top with a victory. We just have those type of players."

Following last night's game, Blaney praised his four freshmen. He commended Denham Brown for his persistent defense on Anthony. He mentioned the bolt of "instant offense" contributed by Anderson's early 3-point streak. And he lauded Armstrong and Brown for broadening the UConn scoring attack.

"To get eight points, seven rebounds from Armstrong and seven points, eight rebounds from White," Blaney said. "Getting 15 and 15 out of the (power forward) spot? That's awesome." ∎

AP TOP 25 POLL

TEAM
1. Florida (50)
2. Arizona (13)
3. Texas (5)
4. Pittsburgh
5. Louisville (4)
6. Kentucky
7. Oklahoma
8. Maryland
9. Duke
10. Notre Dame
11. Oklahoma State
12. Kansas
13. Creighton
14. Wake Forest
15. Marquette
16. Illinois
17. Georgia
18. Connecticut
19. Syracuse
20. Xavier
21. Missouri
22. Alabama
23. Mississippi St.
24. Purdue
25. Stanford
First-place votes in parentheses

BIG EAST STANDINGS

EAST	CONF.	OVERALL
Villanova	6-2	13-8
Connecticut	**5-3**	**14-5**
St. John's	4-5	11-8
Boston College	4-5	11-9
Virginia Tech	3-5	10-11
Providence	3-6	10-10
Miami	2-6	9-10

WEST	CONF.	OVERALL
Syracuse	**7-2**	**16-3**
Notre Dame	7-2	19-4
Pittsburgh	6-2	16-3
Seton Hall	5-4	11-9
West Virginia	3-5	12-8
Georgetown	2-6	10-9
Rutgers	2-6	10-10

BIG NUMBER = 68

Percent Connecticut shot from 3-point range in its last game, an 84-68 win over Providence on Saturday. Ben Gordon led the onslaught, shooting 6 of 8. UConn was 13 of 19 overall.

McNamara's game-winning 3 lifts SU to win over Irish

STORY BY DARRYL SLATER | PHOTOS BY NATALIA JIMENEZ

A half-hour after the fact, even his dad was still searching for the answer.

How, with 26 seconds left and the Syracuse men's basketball team down by one point, did Gerry McNamara get so wide open?

McNamara's game-winning 3-pointer from the right corner gave the No. 17 Orangemen an 82-80 win over No. 10 Notre Dame on Saturday in the Carrier Dome. The win moved Syracuse into first place in the Big East West Division. SU has the best conference record in the league.

McNamara's shot baffled the 32,116 fans — McNamara's father, Gerry, among them.

Gerry approached SU point guard Billy Edelin in the locker room after the game, the question still on his lips: "Why'd they leave him so open?"

Edelin, wide-eyed, mustered the response he'd offered reporters earlier: The play was drawn up for forward Carmelo Anthony, who scored six of his 26 points in a 2:03 span of the second half to lead a 10-0 SU run that tied the game at 69.

"We just went with what we were going with the last five or 10 plays," Edelin told Gerry.

Apparently satisfied, Gerry, wearing a T-shirt emblazoned with the words "McNamara's Band," offered the beaming Edelin a Krispy Kreme doughnut. Gerry brought a box of them from Scranton, Pa. — 52 bus-loads of hometown fans in tow.

"I was surprised (that I was so wide open)," said McNamara, a freshman guard. "But I'm not going to complain."

"On the last play, we were obviously going to go to Carmelo," SU head coach Jim Boeheim said. "They went with a zone (defense), and (Anthony) took the guy in the back of the zone to the basket. And Gerry's standing there."

After a Matt Carroll 3-pointer with 30 seconds left put Notre Dame up, 80-79, SU called timeout. As McNamara left the huddle, assistant coach Mike Hopkins grabbed his jersey and whispered into his ear.

"If you get it," Hopkins said, "rip it."

Edelin, positioned at the top of the key, looked for Anthony and dished a chest pass to McNamara for the game-winner, which fell with 20 seconds left.

The Orangemen almost let the victory slip away. After Anthony hit a layup with 1:31 left, SU led, 79-77. On the next Irish possession, Miller missed a 3, and Carroll fouled Edelin down the court. With a chance to seal the game, Edelin missed both free throws.

"They both felt good," he said. "But they were both on the rim for so long and fell off."

Twenty-eight seconds after the misses, Edelin found McNamara.

"Money," Edelin thought as McNamara's shot sailed through the air.

The Orangemen (17-4, 8-3 Big East) rode Anthony down the stretch, giving the ball to the freshman in the post. If Anthony failed to convert a layup, he drew a foul and went 10 of 10 from the free-throw line.

With the Fighting Irish shying away from double-teaming Anthony, his shots fell easier.

"(Notre Dame head coach) Mike Brey made a statement that they had the best small forward (Dan Miller) in the Big East," Anthony said. "I had to prove him wrong."

"They didn't have anybody who can match him sizewise," Edelin said. "If they tried to put one of their big guys on him, he would go right around him on the dribble."

Early on, the Irish's 3-point shooters dominated. Miller, Carroll and point guard Chris Thomas shot a combined 12 of 25 from 3-point range. Before McNamara's 3, the Orangemen were 2 of 16. For the game, four Notre Dame (19-5, 7-3) players — Carroll (22 points), Torin Francis (17), Thomas (16) and Miller (14) — scored in double figures.

McNamara scored 17 for the Orangemen. Forward Hakim Warrick added 15, and Edelin had 11.

The Orangemen secured the win, in part, by taking care of the ball. SU had four turnovers, compared to Notre Dame's 14. It was the fewest turnovers the Orangemen have committed since they had four in a 1986 Big East tournament game against St. John's.

"To have four turnovers," Boeheim said, "is really unbelievable."

Said Edelin: "When you think about it, Melo had a big second half, and they wanted to make somebody else beat us. And we had no problem doing that." ∎

SEASON PLAY BY PLAY

Admit it: Syracuse is Big East's team to beat

COLUMN BY PETE IORIZZO

Following an 82-80 victory over Notre Dame at the Carrier Dome, a triumvirate of underclassmen from the Syracuse men's basketball team faced a one-question pop quiz.

"Does Saturday's win," the Orangemen were asked, "make Syracuse the Big East's team to beat?"

Answering should be no sweat for three players who've so far demonstrated a basketball savvy well beyond their years, right?

Well, one passed, one failed and the other left the question blank.

"Yeah we're the team to beat," sophomore forward Hakim Warrick said, "especially given the way we play at home. This is one of the toughest places to play. We know we've got a target on our backs."

Right. Warrick passed.

"I'm not going to come out and say that," a grinning Gerry McNamara said. "We're a great team. That's what I can say."

McNamara's game-winning 3-pointer excused him. He escaped with an incomplete. Besides, it's not Golden Boy's personality to trash talk.

That seems more in forward Carmelo Anthony's realm.

"Nope, we will never be the team to beat," Anthony answered defiantly. "We want to be the underdogs."

The naïve freshman better hope for some extra credit. Sooner or later, Anthony will have to fess up to the obvious. No team will take the No. 17 Orangemen lightly. Especially not at home, where Syracuse is 14-0.

Anthony should also study the Big East standings. Thanks to

Pittsburgh hiccuping Saturday and falling to Seton Hall, 73-61, the Orangemen slid into first place in the Big East West Division.

In the East Division, Villanova topped Connecticut, 79-70, on Saturday, meaning with its 8-3 mark, Syracuse has the conference's best record.

If the Orangemen win at Notre Dame on March 4, they have a chance to enter the Big East tournament as the conference's highest nationally-ranked team. That's no small feat considering that, at the season's start, the Associated Press poll ranked Pittsburgh No. 5 and Connecticut No. 15.

Syracuse? It started unranked, mostly because of an inexperienced lineup. Now, SU isn't fooling anyone.

"They're a heck of an offensive team," Notre Dame head coach Mike Brey said. "They've got a lot of guys who know how to take care of the basketball."

That, perhaps, is the most stunning part of this remarkable season. On this Syracuse team, underclassmen aren't just first and second options. They're every option.

Still, Syracuse, which starts two freshmen and two sophomores, routinely shows more poise than its opponents. The Orangemen trailed in eight Big East games and came back to win six.

On Saturday, Notre Dame got 36 points from seniors and 19 from freshmen. The Orangemen's freshmen, meanwhile, contributed 54 points, while lone senior Kueth Duany added just five.

So perhaps it's fitting that McNamara, a freshman, hit the game-winning 3-pointer, while Notre Dame senior Matt Carroll managed only a meager layup attempt that SU center Jeremy McNeil swatted away with five seconds remaining.

More telling, Syracuse coughed up four turnovers to Notre Dame's 14.

Considering the Orangemen's still-wary personas, it's understandable why Anthony wants SU to be anonymous. It's easier to be the team that comes out of nowhere, the one no one overprepares for, the one that, every once in a while, catches an opponent napping.

"We know," Warrick said, "that we're not going to get anything easy now."

Certainly not with that big target on their backs. ■

Orangemen nearly succumb to St. John's scrappiness

STORY BY PETE IORIZZO | PHOTOS BY SETH SIDITSKY

A white bandage bridged Syracuse center Craig Forth's nose after last night's game, making the 7-footer look like a battered prizefighter.

Quite fitting. Scrappy St. John's had just taken the No. 15 Syracuse men's basketball team the proverbial 12 rounds.

Hampered by the Red Storm's quick, physical play, Syracuse needed timely shooting last night to win, 66-60, in front of 21,044 in the Carrier Dome. Syracuse (18-4, 9-3 Big East) improved to 15-0 at home and remains in sole possession of first place in the Big East West division.

Last night, smaller, quicker St. John's players greeted Forth and fellow center Jeremy McNeil with hard swats every time the big men touched the ball. The referees used their whistles sparingly, calling Red Storm players for 17 total fouls, four of which came as St. John's hacked desperately in the last minute.

"Other teams don't swat down and knock at the ball as much," Forth said. "This team does it a lot. They're good at knocking the ball loose."

Forth and McNeil's five combined turnovers were a fraction of the Orangemen's 26, a season high and the most since their 20 in a 73-60 loss at Pittsburgh on Jan. 18. Against Notre Dame on Saturday, SU committed only four giveaways. Syracuse reached that mark four minutes into last night's game.

With 11 minutes remaining in the first half, SU and SJU (12-10, 5-7) had combined for 13 turnovers and 14 points. In total, the game's assist-to-turnover ratio was 21 to 41.

SEASON PLAY BY PLAY

No Orangemen could plead innocent afterward, as none finished with more assists than turnovers. Among the worst offenders was Hakim Warrick, who had six turnovers and zero assists.

But Carmelo Anthony's team-high 21 points and 13 rebounds survived the bevy of turnovers.

"This is probably one of the most physical games I've played in," Warrick said. "The refs let a lot of stuff go."

"We should turn the ball over 15 or 16 times against this team," SU head coach Jim Boeheim said, perhaps realizing the Red Storm entered leading the Big East with a plus-5.67 turnover margin. "If we eliminate those 10 turnovers, it's an eight- or 10-point game."

Especially since St. John's shot 29.3 percent. The Red Storm also went 9 of 41 on 3-pointers, breaking a Big East record for 3-point tries.

"We didn't make shots," St. John's head coach Mike Jarvis said. "Hopefully, the rest of the season, we'll make shots."

For most of the game, the Orangemen failed to make shots, too. They responded with 44.9 percent shooting and attempted 49 shots, their lowest total since the loss at Pittsburgh.

Syracuse's shooting picked up at the most critical juncture, though, especially when a 3-pointer from Kueth Duany tied the score at 51 with 4:58 left.

Duany finished with 17 points. He also hit 2 of 4 from 3-point range and collected six rebounds.

"That's what he's there for," SU point guard Gerry McNamara said. "He's our senior and he's our leader. He led us tonight."

SU badly needed some leadership after the Red Storm broke off a 13-0 second-half run. With 8:49 remaining, Marcus Hatten — who finished with a game-high 22 points on 9-of-25 shooting — capped the run with a 3-pointer to give St. John's a 45-42 lead.

The Orangemen responded by nailing seven consecutive shots to snatch a 58-54 lead with 2:10 left. St. John's cut the deficit to two but never got any closer.

Elijah Ingram's missed 3 at the other end — one of his 18 missed 3-pointers — all but ended the game. St. John's fouled, but SU hit 6 of 7 free throws to sound the final bell.

"That's one of the most physical games we played in," said Anthony, who contributed eight of his 21 during Syracuse's late run. "I saw it against Pitt and Georgetown, but not like tonight." ∎

SEASON PLAY BY PLAY

Oh Shoot! Ingram misses record 18 3-pointers

STORY BY CHRIS CARLSON

When he's on, Elijah Ingram can keep St. John's in a game all by himself. When he's off, Ingram can shoot his team right out of one.

Last night, Ingram shot down the Red Storm's chances in a 66-60 loss to No. 15 Syracuse in the Carrier Dome. The freshman guard tried a conference-record 20 3-pointers. He made just two and missed his final 18. Providence's Donta Wade, who attempted 17 on Feb. 23, 2000, at Notre Dame, held the previous record.

"Ingram… " Syracuse head coach Jim Boeheim mumbled while perusing his stat sheet. "Wow, I didn't even see that one. They can't shoot that well."

In the first half, Ingram made 2 of 10 3-point attempts. He buried the game's first basket, a 3-pointer from the right wing, and made a layup on the next possession.

Then things worsened. He made one of his next two shots, before missing six to end the half.

"You don't count shots during the game," St. John's head coach Mike Jarvis said of his team's Big East-record 41 3-point attempts (The previous record was 38, set by Seton Hall on Jan. 27, 2001, against West Virginia). "You only keep track of good shots. Ninety percent of them were good shots."

Maybe Jarvis should have been counting Ingram's.

St. John's point guard Marcus Hatten had considerable success

penetrating the middle of Syracuse's zone and kicking the ball out to Ingram. Although the SU defense collapsed to stop Hatten, leaving Ingram open, he still struggled.

By the start of the second half, Ingram was already sore. An injured left ankle hampered his shot. He sprained the ankle in

practice Thursday, and the injury forced him to miss Saturday's game against Providence. Ingram also said his legs felt heavy.

Most damaged of all, though, was Ingram's psyche.

"I thought about (taking fewer shots)," Ingram said. "I didn't want to shoot really. But everyone was telling me to keep shooting, keep shooting."

Ingram's shot is ugly. The 166-pound freshman looks like he needs every ounce to hoist his shots. His 3-pointers appear more like hopeless heaves, as his entire body lurches toward the basket.

"We were talking about his shot a lot on the bench," Syracuse freshman Carmelo Anthony said. "But once he gets in a rhythm, he'll make them."

Past experience proves Anthony right. Against Miami on Feb. 2, Ingram made 5 of 7 from 3-point range, leading the Red Storm to a 77-74 win. Entering last night's game, Ingram was shooting 39.3 percent from 3-point range.

If he had equaled his 3-point shooting average, St. John's would have won by 12.

"Every game you lose, you think about the stuff you could have done differently," Ingram said.

Other Red Storm shooters struggled, too. Hatten, the Big East's third-leading scorer, launched 11 3-point attempts and connected on two.

"If the number we took was 41," Hatten said, "we should have made 17 or 19. A lot of them were open looks."

Instead of Hatten's approximated total, the Red Storm made only nine.

"I tell them to keep shooting that damn ball," Jarvis said. "At the end of the game, I was hoping (Hatten) would penetrate, dish the ball out and (Ingram) would make one so we could leave on a positive note."

It didn't happen. Instead, when the ball arrived in Ingram's hands and the game had been decided, he did what he'd done all game. He missed. ∎

Orangemen show moxie in road win over Spartans

STORY BY CHRIS CARLSON | PHOTOS BY AMY YOUNG

EAST LANSING, Mich. — Being the top freshman in the country, a seven-time Big East Rookie of the Week recipient and a sure NBA draft pick weren't enough. Carmelo Anthony still felt he had something to prove.

Entering yesterday's game at Michigan State, Anthony and the No. 15 Syracuse men's basketball team had yet to defeat a quality opponent away from the Carrier Dome. And despite all the accolades heaped upon Anthony, he's constantly questioned about how a freshman can develop the toughness to compete at an elite level.

Yesterday, during Syracuse's 76-75 win over Michigan State in front of 14,759 in the Breslin Center, Anthony provided an answer.

Anthony scored 25 points, including a game-winning 3-point play, against one of the most physical defenses he's seen this season.

"I proved a lot in this win," Anthony said. "We hadn't played well on the road, and Michigan State is one of the most physical teams in the country."

With Syracuse leading, 73-70, Anthony bullied his way toward the basket and stretched to lay the ball in. While Anthony was in midair, Michigan State (14-11) guard Kelvin Torbert cut his legs out from under him, sending Anthony tumbling to the ground. Anthony writhed in pain, rolling on the floor while holding his back.

Since trainers came on the floor to help Anthony, Syracuse (19-4) was charged a timeout. While the Orangemen spent the timeout discussing strategy, Anthony spent it doubled over, stretching his back in various angles.

SEASON PLAY BY PLAY

By the time he stepped to the free-throw line, even Anthony questioned whether he could make the shot.

"I thought I was going to airball it," he said. "I couldn't feel half my body, because it was numb."

Instead, Anthony swished it. The free throw was SU's final point and supplied Syracuse with its slim victory.

"He proved how great he is, and he proved how tough he is," Syracuse point guard Gerry McNamara said. "He makes everyone around him better."

After Anthony's free throw, Michigan State's Chris Hill, who led the Spartans with a season-high 34 points, nailed a 3-pointer from four steps behind the 3-point line. A pair of free throws helped the Spartans climb within a point before their final possession.

With the clock winding down, SU center Craig Forth guarded Torbert, who fired a short jumper. The shot bounced off the rim and was tipped twice before landing in the hands of sophomore Alan Anderson. With two seconds left, Anderson spun and clanged a runner off the rim. As the buzzer sounded, he pulled the bottom of his shirt over his head, hiding his face.

"That's the way the year has gone for us," Michigan State head coach Tom Izzo said. "It was a game we could have won, not saying we should have. But I think we could have."

If they had, Hill could have taken sole responsibility. He nailed a Big Ten-record 10 3-pointers in 18 tries and finished 12-of-20 shooting.

But Hill's exploits weren't enough. Anthony provided Syracuse just enough room. In the first half, Anthony matched Hill shot-for-shot. Three times Hill buried 3-pointers that sent the crowd into a frenzy. Each time, Anthony hushed the fans by returning the favor on the next SU possession. Anthony finished the first half with 15 points, while Hill totaled 17.

Izzo tried myriad defenders on Anthony. He tried zone and

man-to-man defenses. It all failed.

First, MSU tried to use guards to defend Anthony. But SU's freshman dropped 3-pointers over them and backed through them.

"He can bring the ball down the court," said Anderson, who guarded Anthony for portions of the game. "He can pass. There's nothing he can't do."

Izzo eventually called Aloysius Anagonye — a 6-foot-8, 260-pound mound of muscle — to defensive duty. Initially, Anthony challenged the bigger defender, crashing into him on every opportunity.

"I was trying to battle with him," the 6-foot-8, 220-pound Anthony said. "You can't battle with anybody who's that big."

Rather than collect rebounds and points, Anthony collected his first injury of the game.

With 8:47 left in the second half, Anagonye and Anthony battled for a rebound, landed on the floor and exchanged elbows while getting to their feet.

Minutes earlier, Anthony and Anagonye collided while grabbing for a rebound. Anagonye picked up a foul, while Anthony skipped down the sideline, howling in pain and gripping his elbow.

"They threw a lot of stuff at (Anthony)," Boeheim said. "He struggled earlier in the season. He had a few games where he scored 11 or 12 points."

Rather than look flustered, Anthony looked for teammates. Anagonye's effectiveness wore off when Anthony began passing the ball. While collecting all four of his assists in the second half, Anthony proved tough enough to win on the road. He also rid himself of one more pesky question.

"(Anthony's) obviously proved he's a good player over a long stretch," Boeheim said. "He's been a terrific ballplayer all year. If he's shooting well from outside, he's not guardable. I'm not sure if there are two people who can guard him if he makes those." ∎

Spartan's unstoppable Hill breaks 3-point record

STORY BY PETE IORIZZO AND CHRIS CARLSON

EAST LANSING, Mich. — One mistake — a freshman mistake at that — made Syracuse men's basketball head coach Jim Boeheim drop to his knees and beg.

With 1:15 left in No. 15 Syracuse's 76-75 win over Michigan State, the Orangemen led by six points. As Michigan State guard Chris Hill walked the ball up the court, he faked a move to his right. Gerry McNamara took a step back, and Hill planted a 3-pointer from three steps behind the 3-point arc.

After an MSU timeout, Boeheim nearly fell to his knees while lecturing McNamara.

"Gerry, you've got to get out on him, you can't back off," Boeheim said as McNamara walked off the court.

Hill torched SU's zone defense for 34 points, the highest total for an opponent this season and more than double his scoring average of 13.8. Hill had barely scored 34 points in his last four games combined.

Because fellow guard Alan Anderson broke his pinkie finger, Hill is MSU's lone 3-point threat. Yesterday, it was nearly all the Spartans needed.

"(Hill) had an incredible day," MSU head coach Tom Izzo said. "It is so disappointing to see him have a day like that and not be able to feel as good as he should feel."

Hill carried the Spartans in the first half, when he connected on 5 of 7 3-pointers and 6 of 8 field goals. During the first 20 minutes, Hill had 17 points. Ten other teammates contributed 20.

"We left him open too many times," McNamara said. "He hit open shots."

In the second half, Hill finally got a moderate amount of help from his teammates. The Spartans interior passing improved tremendously, and they were able to increase their inside scoring as well as get to the free-throw line more often.

Still, while Kelvin Torbert took MSU's final shot, the Spartans had no questions that Hill should've hoisted the try.

"He had his career-high, we should have come up with a victory," Anderson said. "The final shot was for (Hill) on a double screen."

This time, though, Hill was covered. And Boeheim didn't even have to beg.

NOT SO GOLDEN

Since hitting the clinching 3-pointer against Notre Dame on Feb. 15, Gerry McNamara has stumbled a bit.

Yesterday, McNamara shot 3 of 8 for seven points. He also turned the ball over three times and made only one 3-pointer. Against St. John's last Tuesday, McNamara made 3 of 8 shots and committed a season-high six turnovers.

"I don't know who that was out there," a disappointed McNamara said after the St. John's game. "That wasn't me."

After yesterday's game, McNamara appeared more chipper, though he iced a sore left elbow.

"I was on the ground a couple of times, and I've had a little bit of a bad elbow," the freshman guard said. "So every time I hit the ground, it just adds to it."

JUST FOUL

SU's centers ran into foul trouble again yesterday. Jeremy McNeil fouled out with 4:35 remaining, and Craig Forth finished with four personals. McNeil's early exit was due largely to him picking up three fouls in the game's first nine minutes.

Perhaps because of the foul trouble, Syracuse sometimes used a small lineup. Boeheim first utilized it with 4:15 left in the first half. He went with a three-guard unit of Billy Edelin, Josh Pace and Kueth Duany to play with forwards Carmelo Anthony and Hakim Warrick.

Overall, Syracuse received a seven-point contribution from its centers, on 3-of-3 shooting. McNeil hit his only shot, and Forth made both of his and added a free throw for five points.

THIS AND THAT

Michigan State outrebounded Syracuse, 36-27. Still, the Orangemen scored 32 points in the paint to the Spartans' 22. ... Yesterday marked the first time Michigan State played a non-conference game in the middle of the Big Ten season since Feb. 5, 2000, when it beat Connecticut, 85-66. ... The Orangemen now lead the all-time series against the Spartans, 8-7. Before yesterday, the teams last met in the 2001 Preseason NIT semifinals, with SU winning, 69-58. ... Fans in the Michigan State student section wore white T-shirts with the word "Izzone" ironed on the front, a pun for MSU head coach Tom Izzo's name. ∎

Orangemen defense scales down Mountaineers

STORY BY CHRIS CARLSON | PHOTOS BY DAVID MERRIELL

On a television screen in a dark room, the Syracuse men's basketball team watched the scene repeat over and over.

It was torture. The Orangemen wanted to turn away, but head coach Jim Boeheim demanded fixation on the screen. Repeatedly, one player found soft spots against the SU defense, knocking down a barrage of 3-pointers.

To make his point — that SU needed to play tighter perimeter defense — Boeheim just pushed play. It must have worked, because last night, SU beat up on West Virginia, 89-51, in front of 19,484 at the Carrier Dome.

"Coach didn't let us see the end of it," SU forward Carmelo Anthony said of the tape, which showed Michigan State's Chris Hill dropping 10 3-pointers on the Orangemen last Sunday. "They cut it up, and we were just watching him. They just made a tape of all his shots. We knew we had to do better."

The No. 15 Orangemen (20-4, 10-3 Big East) held West Virginia's primary scoring threats, Kevin Pittsnogle and Drew Schifino, to 19 combined points. The Mountaineer perimeter experts made only 7 of 29 shots, including 2 of 8 from 3-point range.

Schifino was particularly ineffective. The sophomore, who averages 21 points, managed a season-low 10. In the first half, he shot 1 of 9, allowing Syracuse to take a 35-17 halftime lead. Despite his low output, Schifino still led the Mountaineers in scoring.

The 17 points were a season-low for an SU opponent in a half.

"God, that's awful," Schifino said as he perused his stats. "That's awful. That's the worst game I've ever played."

Schifino has Syracuse's tenacious man-to-man defense to thank. After West Virginia started with a pair of 3-pointers against the traditional 2-3 zone, Boeheim banished center Craig Forth to the bench, bringing in freshman Billy Edelin and a new defensive alignment.

Forth and fellow center Jeremy McNeil couldn't keep up with Pittsnogle. Hakim Warrick, though, could. Employing a lineup with no centers, Boeheim placed Warrick on Pittsnogle and senior Kueth Duany on Schifino.

The small lineup harassed the Mountaineers into nine first-half turnovers and 21 percent shooting.

"We can speed them up with the man-to-man," Boeheim said. "You can force some turnovers and not allow them to use all the shot clock. I didn't know we'd play that much man-to-man. Defensively, this was a tremendous effort."

Three times in the first half, WVU failed to score a point during four-minute stretches. With the score 20-14 at the 6:30 mark, Syracuse used the final streak to extend a manageable lead into an insurmountable one.

Anthony began the run, hitting a 3-pointer, but Hakim Warrick provided the capstone on the next possession.

Warrick took a pass from point guard Gerry McNamara, pulled the ball back nearly perpendicular with his body and hammered it through the basket. By the time West Virginia scored again, Syracuse had completed a 10-point run and the Mountaineers failed to get within double figures again.

"When you have a team as inexperienced as ours and you see five shots blocked, five layups blocked, it affects our offense," West Virginia head coach John Beilein said. "They played very good defense. They don't get nearly enough credit for that."

By the start of the second half, the fluxomed Mountaineers rarely penetrated Syracuse's defense. Instead, they became content hoisting 3-pointers, most of which missed. WVU finished 6 of 26 from 3-point range.

The Orangemen, meanwhile, made 14 of 34 shots in the first half. Anthony led Syracuse with 24 points, while Duany and Warrick each totaled 18.

Syracuse's defense made up for an average first-half offensive performance, though.

"That was the best man-to-man defense we've played in a long time," Boeheim said. "The defense really carried us." ∎

100%

84%
CARMELO-METER

A GAME-BY-GAME INDICATION OF
CARMELO ANTHONY'S PERFORMANCE

Twenty-four points and 10 rebounds marks Anthony's 15th double-double this year. But 44-percent shooting is never overwhelming.

God, that's awful. That's the worst game I've ever played.

DREW SCHIFFINO
WV GUARD,
VIEWING HIS
GAME STATS

Inconsistent Edelin glowing about poistive numbers

COLUMN BY ELI SASLOW

It had been a good one, so Billy Edelin beamed in the locker room and joked with reporters. They read him his stats and he smiled. Twenty-five minutes. Ten points. Seven rebounds. Five assists. One turnover.

"Terrific," Edelin said, nodding his head. "It's a good feeling."

Then he turned to laugh with a few kids begging for autographs and poked fun at a teammate. He's learned to appreciate the highs in his Jekyll-and-Hyde season. One game, he'll play for five minutes and fail to score. The next, he'll play for 30 and pack a stat sheet.

In No. 15 Syracuse's 89-51 thumping of West Virginia last night, Edelin played perhaps his most well-rounded game all season. And it left him feeling euphoric.

"A game like this is just great," Edelin said. "I did everything they asked me to do. Some nights, that just doesn't seem to happen, so I enjoy it even more when I play well. I've just been kind of hot and cold."

He's been practically bipolar, a condition SU assistant coach Mike Hopkins attributes to Edelin's year-plus suspension from college basketball.

"You look at the history of kids who have gone through what he has, and they haven't done very well," Hopkins said. "It has to do with the flow of the game. The longer he's back, the more the consistency will come."

Edelin points to a different problem.

"It's minutes," Edelin said. "When I get them, I always play well. If I played 25 minutes a game, I'd do this much or more almost all the time.

But some games, I'll only play five minutes. You just never know what (SU head coach Jim) Boeheim is doing."

Edelin offered no complaints about his minutes for last night's game, though. Boeheim left Edelin on the court for 13 minutes in the second half, pulling him only to put in walk-ons when the game was out of reach.

Edelin's minutes total would likely have been higher had he not bitten through his lip during a battle for the ball midway through the first half. Edelin returned five minutes later but had to receive four stitches in his lower lip after the game. He said the injury won't cause him to miss any practice.

"Billy was very good," Boeheim said. "He helped us on the boards. His defense was good, he made good decisions and he got the ball to people."

Edelin hit 5 of 7 shots. Most of them came in traditional Edelin fashion, a seemingly improbable running heave from just inside the lane.

"He had his best all-around game so far," forward Hakim Warrick said. "He did everything for us. That's what he does for us."

At least some of the time.

WHO'S THAT?

Matt Gorman enjoyed his first playing time since the start of the Big East schedule. The crowd seemed to enjoy it, too.

When Gorman, a freshman, entered the game with eight minutes left, the crowd went wild. When he blocked a West Virginia shot on his first play, the cheers grew louder.

"I guess they like me," Gorman said. "It's definitely nice to have a crowd behind you. I wasn't expecting them to get so loud."

Perhaps Gorman thought the crowd would have forgotten him. Fans hadn't seen him play in 2003. Gorman's last action came when he played 15 minutes and failed to score against Albany on Dec. 28.

"You're not going to put in a freshman who's not ready," Boeheim said. "He's worked hard in practice and lifting, but I can't remember the last time we had a breather to put him in."

Boeheim decided he'd found one with Syracuse up, 66-34, late in the game. Gorman played the last eight minutes, scoring five points and grabbing three rebounds.

A few minutes after Gorman entered, Boeheim cleared his bench. Walk-ons Ronneil Herron, Josh Brooks, Gary Hall, Tyrone Albright and Xzavier Gaines all played.

Herron was the only walk-on to score. He drove to the basket, got fouled, hit the layup and made the free throw to complete the three-point play.

"It's really fun to get out there," Herron said. "The starters love it more than anybody. They're our biggest fans. When I scored, they went crazy."

NO PRACTICE

Syracuse must take today off because of an NCAA rule.

Syracuse plays three games this week, so it is required to take a day off from practice. Since Syracuse practiced Monday and Tuesday, it will take today off, leaving it only Friday to prepare for Saturday's game at Georgetown.

"That's an unbelievable rule," Boeheim said. "I just don't understand it. We only get one day to prepare for Georgetown, which is ridiculous. But we've seen them before, so we'll just go with what we know." ∎

SU beats Georgetown on McNamara's OT heroics

STORY BY CHRIS CARLSON | PHOTOS BY NATALIA JIMENEZ

WASHINGTON, D.C. — He struggled on the road. He struggled with fatigue. He struggled with physical defenses.

And for much of the No. 15 Syracuse men's basketball team's 93-84 overtime victory over Georgetown in front of 17,352 at the MCI Center on Saturday, SU guard Gerry McNamara's difficulties continued.

But over the final seven minutes, McNamara shrugged off each suggestion of his struggles, scoring 14 of Syracuse's final 22 points, including 10 in overtime.

"He never gets any doubt," sophomore Hakim Warrick said. "He's got no memory out there. None. He just keeps shooting. He was struggling, and he's been struggling on the road most of the year, but he came up big down the stretch."

SU's win, coupled with Pittsburgh's victory over Connecticut on Sunday, keeps the Orangemen (21-4, 11-3 Big East) and Pitt tied for first place in the Big East West Division.

McNamara entered Saturday's game connecting on just 21 percent of his 3-point attempts away from the Carrier Dome. He'd also made just 11 of his past 40 3-pointers.

Early on against Georgetown (13-12, 5-9), McNamara's woes continued. He scored two points in the first half and, with 2:17 remaining in the game, he'd shot 1 of 8.

McNamara's fortunes changed when he connected on a 3-pointer — his first basket since SU's first points — to cut Georgetown's lead to 72-71.

"We got him an open look," Syracuse head coach Jim Boeheim said. "Gerry never misses in that situation. Whatever they say (he's shooting lately), I don't want anyone but him taking a 3-pointer at that time of the game."

After burying the 3-pointer to kick-start an 8-2 run, which helped SU take a 76-74 lead, McNamara snuffed out the rally. As the Orangemen attempted to run down the clock, they forced Georgetown to intentionally foul McNamara. With an opportunity to ice the game, McNamara — who missed his first free throw in Big East play earlier in the game — bricked the first of two freebies.

From that point on, McNamara made all his shots. After he hit the second free throw, Georgetown's Gerald Riley buried a 3-pointer, sending the game to overtime. McNamara, though, was determined that his atypical blunder would not cost the Orangemen.

"I had to make up for that foul shot I missed to ice the game," McNamara said. "I got a second chance, so I'm going to put it down the next time."

In overtime, McNamara put down shot after shot.

First, he nailed a free-throw-line jumper. On the next possession, McNamara canned an open 3-pointer as GU double-teamed freshman Carmelo Anthony.

Two possessions later, with Syracuse leading, 85-80, McNamara made good on his second chance to finish off the Hoyas. As the shot clock wound down, McNamara drifted left, sinking a 3-pointer with Georgetown's Brandon Bowman in his face.

McNamara responded with a calm fist pump before a mob of teammates heaped on celebratory high-fives and backslaps.

"I don't think he can make that shot again," Boeheim said, "but he made it."

Said Georgetown head coach Craig Esherick: "Gerry McNamara's shot in overtime was big. He had Bowman all over him. That's NBA, top-of-the-arc type stuff."

To set the stage for McNamara's heroics, Syracuse survived an awe-inspiring performance from Georgetown center Mike Sweetney and a gut-wrenching performance from the Orangemen's offensive options.

Sweetney dominated the game, finishing three assists and three blocks short of a quadruple-double. The Georgetown center led his team in points, assists, rebounds and blocks.

Despite constant double-teams, Sweetney was able to score 31 points by spinning between defenders and tossing up soft jump shots. When not scoring, Sweetney drew two or three defenders and found open teammates.

"He's a good player," Warrick said. "But it's a team game, and we got balanced scoring."

Although Syracuse finished with four players in double figures, it struggled to find any options in the first half. The Orangemen went score-less for the first four minutes. By the time they finally broke the drought, they faced an 11-2 deficit. They finished the half trailing 30-27 and shooting 31 percent on 12-of-38 shooting.

Syracuse was led by Anthony, who nearly matched Sweetney in points with 30, but needed twice as many shots (29) to do it. On offense, the Orangemen stood around, collecting only seven assists and forcing Anthony to attempt awkward shots.

"We couldn't get anything from our offensive sets," Boeheim said. "We were running around like chickens. There were times we didn't know what defense they were in." ∎

Orangemen's comeback script growing tiresome

COLUMN BY DARRYL SLATER

WASHINGTON, D.C. — At 21-4, the Syracuse men's basketball team has a problem: It can't find a simple way to win.

The Orangemen shun easy victories, instead relishing their roles as Comeback Kids. They play by a heart-skipping script that leaves head coach Jim Boeheim pogoing out of his seat on every possession.

Without fail, they'll trail by 10 points in the first half, cut the deficit to five by halftime, blow a couple chances to pull away in the second half and sneak out a win in the final minutes.

It's as predictably tiresome as morning rush hour on the Autobahn.

No. 15 SU followed its comeback trend again Saturday, erasing a 12-point second-half deficit to beat Georgetown, 93-84, in overtime.

"I think we're killing the fans back home," SU center Craig Forth said. "I've heard so many people say, 'Stop making 'em barn burners.' "

By now, SU has torched an Amish community worth of barns.

Saturday marked the 11th time the Orangemen overcame a second-half deficit, and they're 7-3 in games in which they've trailed at halftime.

So, what gives?

"If this were another team, with all the young players we've got," Syracuse forward Carmelo Anthony said, "I don't think they would've won as many games as we've won."

The difference?

"Heart," Anthony said. "Toughness. Never quit."

While Anthony didn't mention that it helps to have one of the country's best player (himself), his four-word season summary sounds a lot like a trailer for a Jerry Bruckheimer film.

After all, this team is a dramedy in high tops. There's controversy (see guard Billy Edelin's 12-game, NCAA-imposed suspension). There's suspense (see speculation about Anthony jumping to the NBA).

But since these are 19- and 20-year-olds, they manage to giggle through tense moments (see Anthony laughing at an airballed a free throw).

"It's kind of like a movie," forward Hakim Warrick said. "I hope we can keep going and get that good-movie ending."

It won't happen, though, if the Orangemen keep following this script.

"We don't mean to get down by 10," Anthony said. "We know that we can't do that in the future, in the tournament."

Indeed, March Madness is where Hollywood tales are crafted or crushed. And SU can only overcome so many 10-point deficits.

But at least for Saturday, Anthony found himself wrapped up in the comeback's tension. He jawed with Georgetown's Gerald Riley, drawing a technical foul. When the Hoyas led by two with 28 seconds left, he bricked two free throws and bit his lower lip as he jogged back down the court.

He knew, of course, that the Orangemen had to make it hard on themselves. They had to prepare their postgame lines about how they'd rather blow teams out but will take a comeback any day.

"We feel like we can come back from anything," Warrick said.

Don't be fooled. These guys love their roles as resurrectors. Last season, SU lacked enough toughness to mount a comeback, but this year, the Orangemen have what Edelin called "that killer mentality."

"Every time we get down," he said, "we just say we're going to find a way to win, just because we've done it before. We find a way to pull it out."

They have to. It's in the script. ∎

SEASON PLAY BY PLAY

Edelin breaks out, scores career-high 26 in SU win

STORY BY DARRYL SLATER | PHOTOS BY JOE PAYMOND

SOUTH BEND, Ind. — One by one, Billy Edelin gathered his Syracuse men's basketball teammates under the basket and grabbed fistfuls of their jerseys. His eyes wide, Edelin screamed something the Orangemen had already realized in the waning minutes of last night's game at Notre Dame.

"They're gonna make a run," Edelin told his teammates. "We've just got to pull together, make some stops and win this game."

The No. 12 Orangemen did. By holding off a late Notre Dame charge and never allowing the No. 16 Irish to take a lead, SU pulled out a 92-88 victory before 11,450 at the Joyce Center. With the win, the Orangemen locked up a first-round bye in the Big East tournament.

Even without his speech — which came with 3:04 left, seconds before a free throw from Notre Dame forward Torin Francis cut SU's lead to 84-83 — Edelin proved a valuable offensive asset. He scored a career-high 26 points on 13-of-20 shooting. Edelin's previous high was 18 in a win at West Virginia.

"I just wanted to try to get everybody focused in," Edelin said of his late-game speech. "I just try to pick my spots, and when (SU head coach Jim Boeheim) gives me the OK to go, I make things happen, don't rush and try to finish.

"I don't take bad shots. I've never played like that. I think it's stupid."

Indeed, Edelin took care of the ball, turning it over just three times in 32 minutes. And he preserved SU's chance to win the game.

Despite being down 11 at halftime, Notre Dame moved within four three minutes into the second half. The Irish whittled away the SU lead, and a 3-pointer from guard Matt Carroll tied the game at 86 with about two minutes left.

A minute later, Notre Dame guard Torrian Jones hit two free throws to tie the game at 88. But on SU's next possession, Edelin made perhaps his most valuable contribution.

With about 50 seconds left, Edelin backed into the lane, searching for a shot. He lost the ball but remained calm and regained possession.

Then, with 39.6 seconds left, SU forward Carmelo Anthony fought his way through traffic and layed in Hakim Warrick's missed turnaround jumper to give SU a 90-88 lead.

Edelin attributed his success to the fact that the Orangemen (22-4, 12-3 Big East) arrived in South Bend on Monday, and he got a chance to sleep all yesterday.

Maybe it's something else, too. After the game, Edelin sported a gray hooded sweatshirt with the words "We R One" on it. Edelin also wore the shirt after SU's last two games, in which he scored 10 and 14 points. When it was suggested that the threads might be lucky, he said, "I guess it might be. I never noticed it."

"Games like this, we needed him out there," Warrick said. "He's patient. He knows what he can do. Once he got a couple easy baskets, that really gets him going."

Boeheim praised Edelin's efforts on Notre Dame point guard Chris Thomas, who had 16 points but shot 7 of 20.

"Billy was really the difference," Boeheim said. "He played pretty good defense. Thomas had to take a lot of shots to get his points. Billy's gone through a lot. He's had to get his game going under tough conditions."

Though Edelin's midseason return from a 12-game, NCAA-imposed suspension slowed his contributions earlier this year, his confidence appears to be brimming. He's looking for his shots more — that runner down the lane is still his favorite — and seems less tentative on defense.

And with Edelin's aggression last night, the Orangemen roared out of the gates instead of falling behind early, which they've done in previous games.

In the first half, SU opened up an 11-2 lead after guard Gerry McNamara hit Syracuse's first two shots, both 3-pointers. McNamara scored 13 of SU's first 21 points and, in the first eight minutes, was 5 of 6, including 3 of 3 from 3-point range.

McNamara finished with 20 points on 8-of-13 shooting, including 4 of 5 from 3-point range.

Carroll led all scorers with 28 points.

The Orangemen grabbed their biggest lead of the game, 39-18, in the first half. But late in the half, Notre Dame (21-8, 9-6) went on a 13-4 run in which it hit three consecutive 3-pointers.

Syracuse went to man-to-man defense for the last two minutes of the first half and started the second that way before switching back to a 2-3 zone.

"I couldn't find the right defense to stop them," Boeheim said. "There may not have been one. We just tried to keep scoring, because neither team really could stop the other team." ■

Slow-starting Anthony comes through in clutch

STORY BY DARRYL SLATER

SOUTH BEND, Ind. — Both words are almost foreign to him, but Carmelo Anthony is sure to make a distinction between "struggled" and "missing."

Anthony, a forward, shot 1 of 5 in the opening eight minutes of the No. 12 Syracuse men's basketball team's 92-88 win over No. 16 Notre Dame last night. He finished with 21 points on 9-of-23 shooting. He shot 1 of 5 on 3-pointers and grabbed 10 rebounds.

When asked if he felt he struggled in the first half, Anthony, a tad irritated, said, "Hell no, man, I wasn't struggling. I was just missing. I wouldn't say that's struggling. They played some tough defense. I'll give them that. But I came through when it counted."

Indeed, Anthony's put-back layup off a missed jumper by forward Hakim Warrick gave the Orangemen a 90-88 lead with 32.6 left. Though Anthony scored seven points in the first half, he made several key plays down the stretch.

With 2:25 left in the game and SU holding an 86-83 lead, Anthony stuffed a shot from Notre Dame guard Torrian Jones. Though the Irish tied the game at 86 with a 3-pointer from guard Matt Carroll, Anthony answered with a driving layup to put SU up 88-86 with 1:32 left.

And while the Irish bumped him, he maintained a measure of poise, something he failed to do last Saturday at Georgetown, when his frustration with physical defense almost reached a boiling point.

"(Notre Dame) was trying to play physical with me," Anthony said. "But I don't think they were used to playing physical."

Said SU head coach Jim Boeheim: "He wasn't able to get much of anything going in the first half. He struggled a little bit tonight."

Anthony's 21 points were his fewest since he scored 21 in a 66-60 SU win over St. John's on Feb. 18. Still, Anthony is seven points away from passing Lawrence Moten's single-season freshman scoring record of 583, which Moten set in 32 games in 1991-92. Should Anthony break that mark in Sunday's regular-season finale against Rutgers, he'd do it in 27 games. And Anthony's 22.2 points per game are four more than Moten averaged in '91-'92.

So after last night's game, Anthony was, well, typical Anthony. He sat shirtless by his locker, joking with roommate and SU guard Billy Edelin as Edelin chatted with a reporter.

Before Edelin was even asked a question about his career-high 26 points, Anthony interjected, "Chris Thomas was too small for him, man," a reference to the Notre Dame guard who defended Edelin.

Later, Anthony was asked about SU's chances of winning next week's Big East tournament in Madison Square Garden. The Orangemen earned a first-round bye with a win last night.

"We're real confident," said Anthony, who scored 27 points in SU's season opener against Memphis in the Garden. "Playing in New York, it's like we're home. What makes me so confident? We're winning right now." ∎

Late rally lifts SU as crowd begs Anthony for one more

STORY BY ADAM KILGORE | PHOTOS BY NATALIA JIMENEZ

A record crowd poured through the Carrier Dome gates Sunday to beg and hope for Syracuse freshman Carmelo Anthony to come back for another season.

He gave them reason to beg, but little reason to hope.

As the deafening chant of "One More Year!" cascaded from the stands onto Jim Boeheim Court during the game's waning seconds, Anthony couldn't help but smile. His 30 points had just lifted SU to an 83-74 victory over Rutgers (12-16, 4-12 Big East) in a game with more subplots than a soap opera.

The win — which came on Senior Day and witnessed the retiring of Sherman Douglas' No. 20 — clinched SU a share of the Big East regular-season title and gave the Orangemen the No. 1 seed from the West Division in next week's Big East tournament. Syracuse ran its home record for the season to 17-0, an unprecedented feat in SU history. An on-campus record 33,071 fans — eclipsing the old mark by 23 — attended.

And oh, by the way, Syracuse (23-4, 13-3) had to overcome a 12-point, second-half deficit to make it all happen.

"For me individually to have 30 points and 14 rebounds, that's a great way to go out," Anthony said. "As a team, to win and go 17-0 at home, that's an awesome way to go out."

A typical way to go out, too. Rutgers led, 54-42, with 13:45 remaining. But Syracuse befuddled Rutgers with its full-court zone press and Anthony scored 14 down the stretch to give SU its 12th victory of the season after trailing in the second half.

"This game was just kind of a microcosm of our season," Boeheim said. "We don't give up. That's the way they are. They battled back all year long."

"People are gonna start calling us the Comeback Kids," Anthony said.

Those fans contributing to the record attendance would like to see Anthony do just that — come back — next year. In what could have been Anthony's final home game, fans brought signs pleading him to return and screamed for another season.

"I got a chill when they were chanting that," Anthony said. "I got a chill through my body."

After the game, Boeheim sent chills through the conference.

"Without a doubt, despite of what some people who don't know anything about basketball think, you saw the best player in the Big East today," Boeheim said, referring to Anthony. "If you don't understand that, I feel real bad for you. He's not going to get it, but if you watched basketball all year long, it's not even close."

Anthony, always cocksure, agreed.

"I know I am," Anthony said. "I know in the back of my mind that I'm not gonna get it. I'm a freshman, man. They don't want to give it to no freshman. I don't think it's fair, but I don't make the calls."

While Anthony may be the player of the year, SU considered guard Josh Pace its player of the game. Coming off the bench, Pace ignited SU's comeback with saran-wrap defense at the head of the press. Victimized by inconsistent playing time much of the year, Pace contributed 10 points, six rebounds and countless headaches to Rutgers point guard Jerome Coleman in 21 minutes.

"He came in when we had no energy, couldn't get anything going," SU assistant coach Mike Hopkins said. "He just made play after play in the press. He's just a tremendous asset to us."

"Josh Pace was the MVP of the game," SU senior Kueth Duany said.

Against a Rutgers team already eliminated from the Big East tournament and playing with no pressure, SU needed Pace's crucial minutes. Rutgers built a 12-point lead in the first half, which the Orangemen erased with a late first-half run.

"Every time we play them, they come out like they have nothing to lose," SU forward Hakim Warrick said.

Undaunted, RU built another 12-point lead behind center Kareem Wright's 10 points in the first five minutes of the second half. Wright scored a team-high 20 despite missing time with an injured right shoulder.

Syracuse stormed back, and Anthony gave SU its first lead, 65-64, since the second minute of the first half by sinking two free throws with 5:36 to play.

Duany and freshman point guard Gerry McNamara drilled consecutive 3-pointers with 1:45 left to give SU a 79-69 lead and ice the game.

After surviving yet another close call, the Orangemen head to Madison Square Garden with utmost confidence. Last year, SU hung their heads at the Big East banquet before the tournament, Warrick said. This year, the spindly sophomore can't wait to get to New York.

"It makes us a lot more prepared," Warrick said. "I'd rather have a close game like this than get a blowout going into the Big East tournament. This year we can go in and hold our head up high and come out with a Big East Championship." ∎

Syracuse boots Hoyas from tourney in typical fashion

STORY BY PETE IORIZZO | PHOTOS BY AMY YOUNG

NEW YORK CITY — Seems a comeback win — especially one where the Syracuse men's basketball team overcomes 15 lead changes and 29 points from Mike Sweetney — should impress head coach Jim Boeheim.

Not with these Orangemen.

"Nothing new," Boeheim ho-hummed. "That's typical of the way we've played all season."

Indeed, No. 1-seeded Syracuse fought back from a second-half deficit for the 13th time this season and beat No. 5 Georgetown for the third time. Throw in last-minute heroics, and the Orangemen's 74-69 win last night in front of 19,528 at Madison Square Garden in the Big East tournament quarterfinals looks much like the typical SU regular-season win.

Last night's victory advanced Syracuse to the semifinals, where it will meet No. 2 Connecticut tonight at 9. The Huskies downed No. 3 Seton Hall, 83-70, last night to advance.

SU has little time to recuperate from the pounding it took from Sweetney, who walked away with game highs in points and rebounds (13). But, for the third time this season, Georgetown's junior center also walked away a loser.

On March 1, Syracuse beat Georgetown, 93-84, in overtime despite 31 points from Sweetney. A month earlier, the Orangemen survived Sweetney's 32 and won, 88-80, at the Carrier Dome.

"I thought this game was going to be an up-and-down game," Sweetney said. "It was, kind of. They slowed it down, packed it in the zone,

This is a real good win for us. It shows us this is just like the regular season.

HAKIM WARRICK
SU FORWARD

basically the same kind of game."

Sweetney hoped for a different kind of ending, and for a while, it seemed he might get it.

The game seesawed during the last 10 minutes, and Syracuse clung precariously to a 68-67 advantage with 37.8 seconds left.

"We've been in this kind of game so many times this season," SU forward Carmelo Anthony said. "I wasn't worried."

Perhaps Anthony's team-high 21 points helped ease his nerves. But SU's defense was the difference.

Leading, 69-67, with less than 30 seconds left, the Orangemen set themselves as the Hoyas walked up the ball. Georgetown worked it around the perimeter until Ashanti Cook flubbed a pass. SU guard Kueth Duany snatched control of the ball, and SU took control of the game following two Gerry McNamara free throws that pushed the lead to 71-67.

Syracuse's second-half comeback was set up by a 41-39 halftime deficit that sprung mostly from Sweetney, who scored 14 first-half points on 6-of-11 shooting.

Even when Sweetney elected not to shoot, the Hoyas' offense moved through his 6-foot-8 presence at the top of the lane. On one possession, Sweetney took the ball near the top of the key, and while the Syracuse defense converged, he dished to Darrel Owens for an open layup, giving the Hoyas a 27-20 lead.

"The first half we were so concerned with Sweetney we were giving other guys some easy shots," Boeheim said. "The second half we did a good job shutting down the other guys."

Indeed, save a Gerald Riley jump shot with 4:13 left, all of Georgetown's 28 second-half points came from either Sweetney or Brandon Bowman. Sweetney totaled 15 in the second half, while Bowman contributed 11 of his 18.

Syracuse compacted its zone after halftime, forcing Sweetney to either shoot from near the foul line or dish to the perimeter. The Hoyas struggled from the outside, shooting 33 percent in the second half compared to 49 percent in the first.

"I thought Syracuse did a really good job on defense of collapsing back on Mike," GU head coach Craig Esherick said, "and really making it very difficult at the beginning of the possession for us to get the ball to Mike. Clearly, we didn't shoot the ball as well as I would've liked on the perimeter."

Said SU forward Hakim Warrick: "We knew they were going to get it to Sweetney. We just wanted to limit what other players could do. We did a good job limiting them in the second half.

"This is a real good win for us. It shows us this is just like the regular season." ∎

Duany learns from previous year's early exit

STORY BY PETE IORIZZO

NEW YORK CITY — The memory still etched in his mind, Kueth Duany warned his teammates.

"Kueth told us about how we lost this game last year and it put us out," SU freshman Carmelo Anthony said. "So that gave us motivation."

Last season, Syracuse lost, to Villanova, in the first round of the Big East tournament. No way would Duany let that happen again. He scored 16 points on 5-of-8 shooting, including 3 of 4 from 3-point range.

Syracuse needed the boost from its lone senior when its offense sputtered through the first half. The Orangemen never got into a flow and seemed unnerved by Georgetown's matchup-zone defense.

But Duany held Syracuse in the game, hitting all three of his first-half shots for 10 points. He also buried both of his 3-point tries.

"They just gave me some open looks," Duany said. "I felt like I had my shot from warm-ups."

"Kueth was tremendous tonight," SU head coach Jim Boeheim said. "We weren't doing anything in the first half, and he hit a couple jumpers."

One after a timeout with 3:04 left brought Syracuse within three. Then, following two Georgetown free throws, Duany drilled an NBA-range 3-pointer to cut the Hoyas' lead to 36-34.

But Duany's biggest play came late in the second half. With 22 seconds left and Syracuse clinging to a 69-67 lead, he was credited with a steal.

To Boeheim it looked more like a gift. Replays showed the ball slipped out of Georgetown guard Ashanti Cook's hands as he attempted a pass.

"I'm not giving him credit for that steal," Boeheim quipped. "You'd have to be listening on the radio to give him that one."

OFF NIGHT

Gerry McNamara needed few words to describe his performance.

"I played awful," the freshman guard said.

McNamara made just 1 of 5 shots and missed his three 3-point attempts. Worse, he turned the ball over four times, including three in the first half.

"He struggled a little bit," Boeheim said. "He left his feet a little bit and never really played his game."

Said McNamara: "(Boeheim) said, 'Don't worry about it.' I said, 'I'll be ready (tonight),' and he said, 'I know you will.' "

Before tonight, McNamara will try to relieve the swelling in his sore right elbow. He injured it against Michigan State on Feb. 23 and aggravated it in the second half last night when he was steamrolled while attempting a layup.

After writhing in pain for a moment, McNamara stood up, flexed his elbow a few times and headed to the free-throw line. The 93 percent free-throw shooter missed both, drawing gasps from the crowd.

McNamara denied the elbow had anything to do with the misses.

"No," McNamara said without hesitation. "I don't want to talk about the misses."

RUNNER UP

Despite some last-minute campaigning from Boeheim, Anthony finished second Tuesday in Big East Player-of-the-Year voting. Troy Bell, Boston College's point guard, won the award.

Boeheim made a pitch for Anthony following Syracuse's win against Rutgers on Sunday, but it failed to sway enough Big East coaches.

Anthony did, however, win Rookie-of-the-Year honors. He averaged 22.5 points and 10 rebounds this regular season and set a conference record by winning the Rookie-of-the-Week award 10 times.

THIS AND THAT

Georgetown forward Gerald Riley unintentionally poked Anthony in the eye with 2:25 left in the game. Anthony paced the floor and rubbed his eye, and SU called timeout to give him time to recover. Anthony never came out of the game and afterward said the eye felt fine. ... Syracuse beat Georgetown three times in a season for the first time in school history. ... SU upped its all-time Big East tournament record to 34-20, second best in the conference. ... The Orangemen donned their home whites last night. Quite fitting, considering the SU fans easily outnumbered and drowned out the Georgetown faithful. The Syracuse band also performed the national anthem. ■

SEASON PLAY BY PLAY

High-speed Huskies knock off Syracuse in semifinals

STORY BY PETE IORIZZO | PHOTOS BY AMY YOUNG

NEW YORK CITY — Turns out this Syracuse men's basketball team is mortal, after all.

The top-seeded Orangemen lost for the first time in eight games last night, falling, 80-67, to second-seeded Connecticut in front of 19,528 at Madison Square Garden in the Big East Championship semifinals. Having been ousted from the conference tournament, SU will learn Sunday how much the loss hurts its NCAA Tournament seeding.

Connecticut, meanwhile, will face No. 2-seeded Pittsburgh tonight at 8 in the finals. The Panthers downed top-seeded Boston College, 61-48, last night to advance.

"This was the first game our youth really showed," SU head coach Jim Boeheim said. "We'll learn from this."

The Orangemen failed to learn from their regular-season game against the Huskies.

On Feb. 10, Connecticut handed Syracuse its most lopsided loss of the season, 75-61, in Hartford, Conn. The Huskies had four players score in double figures to overcome a then-career-high 29 points from SU freshman Carmelo Anthony.

The same theme developed last night. Again, Anthony scored 29, and again, four Huskies scored in double figures. Rashad Anderson led UConn with 21 points.

Of Syracuse's 80 shots, Anthony tried 28, hitting nine. He also collected 15 rebounds.

SEASON PLAY BY PLAY

The rest of the Orangemen combined to shoot 14 of 52. Among the worst offenders were guards Gerry McNamara (1 of 7) and Kueth Duany (2 of 10).

Duany, SU's lone senior, had sparked Syracuse against Georgetown a night earlier, scoring 16 points. But like the rest of the Orangemen, he struggled against a physical UConn defense.

"We tried to take away everything else," Connecticut coach Jim Calhoun said, "and do the best we could on Carmelo Anthony."

Offensively, Connecticut hurried the pace, quickly transitioning Syracuse misses and rarely setting up a half-court offense.

In the first half, the Orangemen's press slowed the Huskies. But in the second, Connecticut ran through it, posting 24 points in less than nine minutes.

"They just have good ball-handlers," Duany said. "It's tough to press a team that has three guards who can handle the ball."

"We tried to be real aggressive pushing the ball up and getting easy baskets," UConn guard Taliek Brown said. "We tried to not even get in a half court. We figured if we could get easy baskets, why not?"

SU center Jeremy McNeil did his best to limit UConn's easy baskets, blocking a Big East tournament-record eight shots. But he picked up his fourth foul with 10:59 remaining and had to be removed.

Soon after, the game spiraled out of the Orangemen's reach, as the Huskies pushed the lead to 66-47 midway through the second half.

"They didn't really attack us like we thought they would," Brown said. "That made it easier."

It looked like it might not be so easy for the Huskies following a Jekyll-and-Hyde first half that was, for each team, part horror show, part highlight reel. UConn led 36-27 at the break.

The Huskies spurted first, tearing off a 19-4 run that jolted them to a 26-10 advantage. Syracuse scored just one field goal during UConn's run, an Anthony layup that made the score 16-9.

Anthony tried to take control, attempting 15 first-half shots. But he hit just four for 11 points.

Overall, SU shot 21.4 percent in the first half. For Syracuse, only Anthony converted more than one field goal, as the rest of the Orangemen combined for 5-of-27 shooting.

When SU pressed following a timeout with 7:36 left, though, it threw off the Huskies. McNamara started Syracuse's retaliation with a steal that led to an Anthony dunk. Two possessions later, McNamara buried a 3-pointer after the Syracuse press forced Connecticut to throw a pass out of bounds.

"We did as good a job as we could in our press to fight back," Boeheim said, "but we probably had to expend a lot of energy doing it."

With 2:38 remaining, the Orangemen had closed the score to 28-24 thanks to a 14-2 run. But UConn responded with a 5-0 spurt to end the half.

"We've got some young guys playing in their first Big East tournament," Boeheim said. "We didn't play well either night here. That's not unusual for a young team." ■

SEASON PLAY BY PLAY

SU holds off feisty Jaspers in NCAA Tournament opener

SEASON PLAY BY PLAY

STORY BY CHRIS CARLSON | PHOTOS BY AMY YOUNG

BOSTON — After an average win against an average tournament team, the Syracuse men's basketball team said all the right things.

Manhattan was a tough team. Manhattan battled. Manhattan played with heart.

"They were a scrappy little team," SU freshman Carmelo Anthony said.

But masked in Anthony's small compliment was big meaning.

During No. 3-seeded Syracuse's 76-65 win over No. 14 Manhattan on Friday afternoon in front of 18,141 at the Fleet Center, the Jaspers weren't scrappy enough. And as Anthony said, they were far too little.

With the win, Syracuse advances to a second-round meeting with Oklahoma State on Sunday afternoon at 2:40.

Syracuse used its size advantage against Manhattan, shooting 58 percent from the field, blocking nine shots and outrebounding the Jaspers, 39-28. While the Orangemen grabbed an offensive rebound every other shot, Manhattan earned a second chance one of every four opportunities.

"We got overwhelmed a little bit," Jaspers coach Bobby Gonzalez said. "We got out-classed a little bit by Syracuse today. They're just a little too big for us on the boards."

In the first half, Syracuse struggled to take advantage of its height-deprived opponents. Anthony, whose bullish figure gave him a physical edge, was content to test his jump shot, leading to 3-of-8 first-half shooting.

Although SU head coach Jim Boeheim half-joked, half-attempted to relieve the pressure on his star freshman by blaming Anthony's interior ineffectiveness on "bad coaching," Anthony said he was just checking his range.

"I was trying to see where my (jump shot) was at outside," Anthony said. "Now I know I have to go inside and then out."

Seldom-used guard Josh Pace used his size to help the Orangemen to a 35-31 halftime lead. Pace, who averages 3.5 points, nearly doubled that number in the first half. On three occasions Pace, who finished with

We got overwhelmed a little bit. We got out-classed a little bit by Syracuse today. They're just a little too big for us on the boards.

BOBBY GONZALEZ
MANHATTAN
COACH

eight points, took the ball outside, bumped his defender below the free-throw line and buried unobstructed jump shots.

"I though Josh Pace was terrific in the first half" Boeheim said. "When he gets (inside), he's a finisher. It's been a tough two years for him, not being able to play much. He's better than we hoped he'd be at this stage of the year."

As the Orangemen's inside presence grew, so did their lead. Anthony scored 10 of his team-high 17 in the second half, using strong interior moves. Point guard Billy Edelin also backed into the paint, making one move and spinning his way to 15 points on 6-of-9 shooting.

"A guy like Billy Edelin comes off the bench, and he's a 6-foot-4 point guard," Gonzalez said. "We have no matchup for him. We are quick little guys. He's just a tough matchup."

With 6:57 left, Manhattan trimmed SU's lead to 61-56 before Anthony responded, scoring six of SU's next eight points.

"The whole team was telling me to go inside, not only coach," Anthony said. "In the second half, I took advantage of the situation."

Jared Johnson led the Jaspers with 22 points, while star guard Luis Flores pitched in 20.

Despite three Manhattan second-half runs — keyed by Johnson and Flores — that cut SU's lead to five points or less, senior Kueth Duany said the Orangemen never felt they could lose the game.

No matter how quickly Syracuse's lead shrunk, its height advantage remained.

"We had a size advantage at every position," Duany said. "That's something you just have to take advantage of." ∎

Down 17 early, SU rallies again to make Sweet 16

STORY BY CHRIS CARLSON | PHOTOS BY AMY YOUNG

BOSTON — For 13 minutes, the Syracuse men's basketball team appeared ready to reaffirm the myth it spent all season obliterating.

The one that said young teams are too tender and mistake-prone to win important games. The one SU had been questioned about throughout the year. The one that said pressure situations would coat their hands in sweat and turn their legs to pudding.

But after falling behind early against Oklahoma State in front of 18,389 yesterday at the FleetCenter, the No. 3-seeded Orangemen turned the No. 6 Cowboys into the bumbling ball-handlers during a 68-56 second-round NCAA Tournament win.

With the win, Syracuse (26-5) moves on to the Sweet 16. The Orangemen will meet No. 10 Auburn at the Pepsi Arena in Albany at 9:40 p.m. Friday. The Tigers advanced yesterday by beating No. 2 Wake Forest, 68-62.

Facing a 25-8 deficit to OSU (22-10) early on yesterday, Syracuse head coach Jim Boeheim resorted to a full-court press and a trio of reserves to turn the game around.

"Desperation," Boeheim said. "That was the desperation press. When you're 17 down and not going anywhere, you have to do something to get your team back in there.

"I was thinking of a tee time for next week."

After instituting the press, SU wasn't desperate for long. The pace of the contest changed from a trudging march to a breakneck sprint. With their offense sped up, the Cowboys committed five turnovers over the final 7:34 of the half and saw their lead cut to 31-25 at halftime.

"As I told (my team) at halftime, 'Guys, if you continued to play like you had, you had a 20-point lead,'" Oklahoma State head coach Eddie Sutton said. "We certainly should have had a double-figure lead at halftime."

Stuck in a half-court game for most of the first half, the SU offense struggled. OSU's vaunted defense pressured the Orangemen into eight turnovers before the 11:00 mark.

When the Orangemen managed to attempt a shot, they were rushed and well defended. Forwards Hakim Warrick and Carmelo Anthony hoisted fading attempts while guard Gerry McNamara failed to find his 3-point shot.

"They made me force my shots early," Anthony said. "They made me play like a freshman."

McNamara agreed that the OSU defense embarrassed the Orangemen early.

"We fell right into their hands," McNamara said. "I rushed shots and didn't do what a guard is supposed to do."

After falling behind 25-8, Syracuse ended the first half on a 17-6 run, keyed by the press and the output of backup guards Josh Pace and Billy Edelin. Pace and Edelin combined to score 16 of SU's final 20 points of the half.

It was the second consecutive game in which the Orangemen's backups sparked them. During a 76-65 win over Manhattan on Friday, Pace and Edelin scored most of their 23 combined points while helping Syracuse pull away.

Yesterday, Syracuse needed the pair just to stay close.

With 6:17 left in the half, OSU began to feel the pressure of SU's press. Within four minutes, Syracuse hurried the Cowboys into three turnovers, while converting three layups and a pair of jump shots. Pace and Edelin scored four consecutive baskets during the run.

In the second half, the press became even more effective. Syracuse only scored six points off nine turnovers, but the press forced the Cowboys into a number of full-speed charges at SU center Jeremy McNeil.

McNeil generally got the best of the collisions. He picked up three of his four blocks in the second half, frightening the Cowboys away from the paint. On his first block of the second half, McNeil swatted a Melvin Sanders layup attempt into the second row. Four minutes later, he rejected a jump shot by Tony Allen.

McNeil's blocking acumen made an impression. For the rest of the game, OSU attempted awkward layup attempts and avoided McNeil rather than driving to the rim. After McNeil's second block, the Cowboys missed 11 shots from within six feet of the basket.

"If any other player was back there, we'd say we just gave (a basket) up," Warrick said. "Not with Jeremy back there. You could just see it. They couldn't believe when they came back."

While McNeil held the Cowboys down defensively, Anthony and McNamara found their offense. The pair combined to score 25 of Syracuse's 43 second-half points.

Anthony, who had been stifled by the presence of Sanders, OSU's defensive stopper, and three first-half fouls, broke loose by heading to the basket. Anthony and McNamara keyed a 17-4 offensive spurt, turning a six-point deficit into a seven-point lead.

With 12:35 left, Anthony gave Syracuse its first lead, freezing a defender with a stutter step and hitting a 3-pointer. Moments later, after a Pace block, Anthony drove past a defender and converted a layup. McNamara finished the run, nailing a 3-pointer from the right corner. After that shot, Oklahoma State failed to get within four points the rest of the game.

"I told myself at halftime that I wasn't going out like this, I wasn't ending my season like this," Anthony said. "Then, in the huddle before the second half, I told the team I owed them a half."

The win continues to showcase Syracuse's ability to come back from uninspiring starts and nearly devastating deficits. Syracuse has come back to win eight games after trailing at halftime.

"This was a tremendous effort," Boeheim said. "To come back from 17 points down against a good team is very hard, especially with young guys. There might be some truth to the fact that these guys are too young to know they're in trouble, but I don't think that's true. These guys just want to keep winning." ∎

High-flying Warrick grounded by strange illness

BY CHRIS CARLSON

BOSTON — Hakim Warrick finally found something that could keep him weighted to the ground — even if he's not sure what it is.

During this weekend's NCAA Tournament wins over Manhattan and Oklahoma State, Syracuse men's basketball fans weren't treated to the usual array of highlight-reel dunks and tape-measure leaps because Warrick, a sophomore, struggled through both games with what he called a "weird virus."

The illness relegated Warrick to his bed for three days and brought him a fever of 102 degrees.

"He just stayed in bed and kept his blanket over his head," said sophomore Josh Pace, Warrick's roommate for the trip. "He didn't feel good, and he didn't want any of us to get sick either."

Warrick was held out of practice for several days before the tournament.

Against the Cowboys, Warrick played 37 minutes but scored only 11 points. In the first-round victory over Manhattan, Warrick played 16 minutes. After a turnover and a pair of mental mistakes in the first three minutes, SU head coach Jim Boeheim yanked Warrick for the rest of the half.

Warrick fared better in the second half, taking advantage of a huge height advantage to score all 10 of his points.

Still, he looked nothing like a potentially dominating power forward. Instead of dunking, Warrick settled for jump shots and layups.

Boeheim said Warrick felt better before yesterday's contest but still wasn't 100 percent.

"Hakim's still struggling a little bit," Boeheim said. "Hopefully he'll be back to full strength next week."

KNOCKED STRAIGHT

With poor performances in both Big East tournament games, a poor NCAA Tournament debut and a dud of a first half against Oklahoma State, one had to wonder what was wrong with SU freshman guard Gerry McNamara.

Boeheim shot down suggestions of McNamara hitting a "freshman wall," often stating: "That's an NBA thing. I've never heard about that in college basketball."

Apparently, all McNamara needed was a stiff knock on the noggin.

Until the second half of Friday's game against Manhattan, McNamara had shot 6 of 21 in the postseason, including a putrid 2 of 12 in the Big East tournament.

Yesterday, McNamara looked poised to continue the trend, missing all six of his shots in the first half.

"Gerry is Gerry, he's a big-game player," Boeheim said. "He can miss 10 in a row, but he's going to make the big shots."

With 14:24 left in the second half, McNamara absorbed an accidental elbow and then a head-butt from OSU guard Victor Williams. With blood trickling into his right eye, McNamara buried a 3-pointer to give SU its first lead of the game.

"I don't think my right eye was working too good," McNamara said. "I used the left eye to shoot. I was wobbly so I tried to get my legs into it a little more."

Officials immediately stopped the game, sending McNamara off the court until he stopped bleeding.

He just stayed in bed and kept his blanket over his head.

JOSH PACE
WARRICK'S
ROOMMATE
FOR THE TRIP

SEASON PLAY BY PLAY

Minutes later, Boeheim rose from the bench and demanded that someone "go get Gerry. I need him now."

"I don't have much patience for medical people," Boeheim said.

With a circular bandage covering the cut — which would need two stitches after the game — McNamara finished the game 5 of 13, making 4 of 10 3-point attempts.

"Once he got hit in the head, he started to play better," Boeheim said. "I guess we'll just have to hit him a little earlier next time."

THIS AND THAT

With the win, Syracuse improved the Big East's record to 8-0 in this year's NCAA Tournament. Connecticut, Pittsburgh and Notre Dame all advanced to the Sweet 16. ... Sophomore guard Josh Pace's 27 minutes marked the third consecutive game in which he's played double-digit minutes. That hadn't happened since Jan. 18. ... Syracuse began the second half without its regular starting lineup on the floor for the first time this season. Senior guard Kueth Duany and sophomore center Craig Forth were replaced by junior Jeremy McNeil and freshman Billy Edelin. ■

SU holds off Auburn, will meet Oklahoma in Elite 8

STORY BY DARRYL SLATER | PHOTOS BY NATALIA JIMENEZ

ALBANY — Ten minutes into the Syracuse men's basketball team's game last night against Auburn, Oklahoma assistant coaches Bennie Seltzer and Jim Shaw were already discussing defensive matchups for a potential Orangemen-Sooners matchup in Sunday's Elite Eight.

As Seltzer munched on a sub and downed Mountain Dew, he scribbled notes on a yellow legal pad, diagramming a hole in the middle of SU's zone and noting SU center Jeremy McNeil as a "BT (big time) shot-blocker." By halftime, he had three times more notes on SU than on Auburn.

After all, the Orangemen jumped on the Tigers early, so much so that Seltzer remarked to Shaw about Auburn playing with "no energy."

Despite a late Auburn charge, the No. 3-seeded Orangemen continued their storybook season, outlasting the No. 10 Tigers, 79-78, in the NCAA Tournament's Sweet 16 in front of 15,093 at the Pepsi Arena.

Syracuse advanced to the Elite Eight for the first time since 1996, when it eventually lost to Kentucky, 76-67, in the national championship game. The Orangemen will play No. 1 Oklahoma tomorrow at 2:40 p.m. The Sooners beat No. 12 Butler, 65-54, earlier last night.

Carmelo Anthony led SU (27-5) with 18 points and eight rebounds. Three other Orangemen — Hakim Warrick, Josh Pace and Kueth Duany — scored in double figures. Warrick had 15, Pace had a career-high 14 and Duany scored 12.

Forward Marquis Daniels shot 12 of 21 for 27 points to lead the Tigers (22-12). Nathan Watson added 16 and shot 4 of 7 on 3-pointers.

"We felt in control the whole game," Warrick said.

With their confidence buoyed by a pro-SU crowd, the Orangemen jumped out to a 10-2 lead. After a Warrick turnaround with 4:09 left in the first half, SU owned a 17-point advantage, its largest of the game.

Down 37-27 at the half, Auburn stormed back, cutting SU's lead to four in the first 4:12 of the second half. Syracuse eventually stretched its lead to six with 42 seconds left, but the Tigers refused to fade.

Lewis Monroe's 3-pointer with 30 seconds left cut the score to 73-70. Duany hit two free throws with 13 seconds remaining to give the Orangemen a five-point lead. Five seconds later, Auburn's Watson nailed a 3. But on the next SU possession, Anthony threw a half-court inbounds pass to Pace, who raced down the court for a dunk to ice the game.

Pace's slam was fitting, considering the burst of energy he provided SU.

"I just wanted to hurry up and get the game over," Pace said of the Tigers' late run.

Said Warrick: "(Pace) really sparked us. When he's scoring like that, it really lifts the burden off Carmelo."

For the second straight game, Anthony struggled in the first half, shooting 0 of 4. Duany made up for Anthony's struggles, scoring eight of SU's first 10 points.

Pace first entered the game with about seven minutes left in the first half. He played 22 minutes, five fewer than he logged in the Orangemen's second-round win over Oklahoma State last Sunday. In Big East games this year, Pace played more than 20 minutes twice.

"I just try to be ready," Pace said. "There's really no way you can stay warm. You can't have a bicycle over there. It's just (that I'm) seeing more minutes. I was telling myself to be more aggressive."

Pace proved especially effective in the second half, when the Tigers employed a triangle-and-two defense to try to slow Anthony and guard Gerry McNamara.

"We got a like out of synch when they went with the triangle-and-two," SU head coach Jim Boeheim said. "Josh made some key plays in there. We just had to find a way to hang on." ■

SU headed to New Orleans after romp of Oklahoma

STORY BY DARRYL SLATER | PHOTOS BY NATALIA JIMENEZ

ALBANY — On Friday night, Oklahoma assistant coaches Bennie Seltzer and Jim Shaw thought they'd found a hole in the Syracuse men's basketball team's 2-3 zone defense.

As the coaches scouted the Orangemen's Sweet 16 game against Auburn, Seltzer scribbled notes on a yellow legal pad, circling what he thought was a weak part of the defense.

Yesterday, the Sooners found few holes. Syracuse's defense stayed active, holding Hollis Price, Oklahoma's leading scorer, to eight points as the No. 3-seeded Orangemen beat the No. 1 Sooners, 63-47, in the NCAA Tournament's Elite Eight before 15,207 at the Pepsi Arena.

Syracuse advanced to the Final Four for the fourth time. It will play Texas in the Superdome in New Orleans on Saturday.

"Our defense was the difference," SU head coach Jim Boeheim said. "We were very active on the defensive end. It's probably the best we've played all year. We did a good job of making them shoot tough shots."

Indeed, the Sooners (27-7) shot 31 percent, with Price going 3 of 17, including 2 of 11 from 3-point range. Oklahoma's 47 points are the fewest SU (28-5) has allowed all year. The Sooners tallied 20 points in the first half and failed to score in the second half until Price hit a 3 with 14:59 left.

"We knew their offense goes through Hollis Price," SU forward Carmelo Anthony said. "He's the driver of their car. Once we took him away, everything just broke down."

Said SU guard Kueth Duany: "It seemed like they were trying to be

real patient. I think they were over-patient, and it took them out of their rhythm. It just hurt their offense when they tried to wait too long to go."

Several times, Oklahoma waited until fewer than 10 seconds remained on the shot clock before it tried to drive to the hoop.

SU's defense proved pesky enough to force 19 turnovers. The Sooners turned the ball over on three straight first-half possessions, allowing the Orangemen to stretch their lead to 10-3. Syracuse led by as many as 18 points in the second half.

Forward De'Angelo Alexander led the Sooners with 14 points, on 5-of-9 shooting.

Anthony had 20 points and 10 rebounds for the Orangemen, and forward Hakim Warrick scored 13.

As the clock ticked down and the Orangemen's victory drew closer, Anthony pointed toward the stands, where his mother, Mary, and advisor, Troy Frazier, sat. Chants of "Final Four!" erupted from the SU student section. When Anthony was announced as the East Regional's Most Outstanding Player, the pro-Syracuse crowd chanted "One More Year!"

The chants continued when Anthony cut down the net, which he wore over his backward hat in a postgame press conference.

"That's my boy," a beaming Mary said.

One section over, Boeheim's wife, Juli, cupped her hands around her mouth and yelled to her husband: "I love you." As Boeheim held his son, James III, a broad smile crossed his face.

The joy struck Boeheim's assistants, too. Stoic associate head coach Bernie Fine, Boeheim's 27-year right-hand man, wept as the buzzer sounded. Assistant Mike Hopkins carried his son, Michael Griffith Jr., and whispered, "We're champions, buddy," into his tot's ear.

Later, the Orangemen reflected on the win, which they counted as one more step in proving their critics wrong.

"It's a great feeling being here as everybody thought we were gonna be a bad team this year," guard Josh Pace said. "Throughout the whole season, nobody gave us respect. We lost our first game (70-63 to Memphis), and that gave people more fuel to throw on the fire."

Said center Craig Forth: "Based on what everybody was saying, we weren't thought to do much of anything. Now, here we are. And maybe we did play with a chip on our shoulder the whole time, kind of expecting to win." ∎

Anthony adds prophet to his first-year resume

COLUMN BY DARRYL SLATER

ALBANY — The Prophet soaked in his success here yesterday, smiling for the TV lights, celebrating for photographers and playfully performing all those other acts that make him the media's Wonder Boy.

Even when a reporter hit Carmelo Anthony with a question he dodged the last two weeks, the prized freshman's ears perked. Syracuse's heart beats, after all, at his pace. When he plays well, the Orangemen play well. When he gets excited, they do, too.

So when he recalls his declaration, they must, too.

Remember, Carmelo, that guarantee you made after Syracuse's win at Notre Dame on March 4? Remember how you said, "You heard it from my mouth: If we get a No. 3 seed, get your Final Four tickets"?

Of course you do.

"You were the one I told that to," Anthony said, referencing the story that appeared in this paper.

The Prophet paused and grinned.

"I came through," he said.

And he did so with his typical gusto, scoring 20 points and 10 rebounds to make good on the guarantee. The No. 3-seeded Orangemen advanced to the NCAA Tournament's Final Four with a 63-47 win over Oklahoma.

"Whoever said we weren't gonna go, they've got to eat their words," SU guard Kueth Duany said. "Carmelo was 100 percent right."

He let the world know yesterday. He threw Final Four T-shirts into the crowd after the game. In a postgame press conference, he showed up with a freshly sheared net pulled snugly over his backward Final Four hat.

But Anthony left everyone wondering again, remaining mum on whether he'll jump to the NBA after this year.

"This is my first Final Four," Anthony said. "And, hopefully, it won't be my last."

Anthony's roommate, SU guard Billy Edelin, knows Anthony's routine and called him "a big kid."

"He better be thanking us," Edelin joked about Anthony's guarantee, "because people would be getting on his back right about now if we'd lost.

"(Making the Final Four) probably justified why he came to college. All that he wanted to come for was this."

Anthony's play early yesterday showed why. Though he's struggled in the first half of late, he scored 12 points in that half against Oklahoma.

"He hadn't played a full great game, but he did that," Duany said. "He made a couple jump shots early that he hadn't made. That got our juices flowing early."

Like always, he led and they followed. Anthony's energy sparked the Orangemen, who stretched their lead to as many as 18 points in the second half by relying on Anthony to dismantle the Sooners' man-to-man defense.

Perhaps that's why, during an interview with CBS earlier in the weekend, oft-curmudgeonly SU head coach Jim Boeheim told Anthony, "I love you."

"I was shocked," Anthony said.

Well, Anthony's shocked everybody. Not so much with his game as with his brash demeanor, unfitting of a freshman.

"A lot of people say freshmen can't take a team to the Final Four," he said. "But we did it."

Anthony's days as The Prophet are finished. His guarantee brought the Orangemen this far. The rest, of course, still depends on him. ∎

Anthony's dominant effort sends SU to title game

STORY BY PETE IORIZZO | PHOTOS BY AMY YOUNG

NEW ORLEANS — Whatever was said, Carmelo Anthony decided it needed no answer. A career-high 33 points and 14 rebounds, he figured, said it all.

So when Texas coach Rick Barnes barked at Anthony each time he came down the court in the second half Saturday, Anthony declined to indulge him in conversation.

"I don't really know what he was saying," Anthony said. "I was just laughing at him."

Indeed, Anthony's ravaging of Texas' defense was laughable. He carried the No. 3-seeded Syracuse men's basketball team to a 95-84 win over No. 1 Texas in front of 54,432 at the Louisiana Superdome. The win vaulted Syracuse (29-5) into the national championship game for the first time since 1996.

The Orangemen face Kansas here tonight at 9:22. The Jayhawks advanced by pummeling Marquette, 91-64, before SU's game Saturday.

"It doesn't get much better than this," Anthony said. "Playing in the national championship game? That's like the biggest event besides the Super Bowl."

Anthony had plenty of help Saturday, as four Orangemen scored in double figures. Brandon Mouton led Texas (26-7) with 25 points.

As the final seconds ticked off the clock, Anthony, standing near the Texas bench, pumped his fists and looked toward the crowd. He saw a band of orange-clad fans bouncing up and down. Ten minutes after the game, chants of "Let's Go Orange!" rang through the Superdome's bowels.

Anthony had given fans good reason to celebrate. He easily discarded several Texas defenders in reaching the 30-point plateau for the first time since March 9, when Syracuse beat Rutgers in its regular-season finale.

Texas guard Royal Ivey, a member of the Big 12's All-Defensive Team, failed to slow Anthony, allowing him to reach 20 points with 18 minutes left in the game. Midway through the second half, Barnes switched and tried Mouton, who quickly fouled Anthony twice in one possession.

"I thought they'd put a bigger guy on me, rough me up a bit and try to get five fast fouls on me," Anthony said. "They didn't do that, though."

Instead, the 6-foot-8 Anthony muscled into position for easy baskets. Other times, Anthony simply pulled up and extended over Ivey (6-3) and Mouton (6-4).

"He's a great player," Mouton said. "He knows how to use his body to get shots. But it's more than a one-man show. They play well as a team."

That showed during a key second-half run. It started, innocently enough, with two free throws from Josh Pace to give SU a 63-61 lead. Then came a Gerry McNamara 3. Then an awe-inspiring Hakim Warrick dunk. Next a McNamara jumper, and the Orangemen had taken a 70-63 lead.

"We have other guys that are really capable, guys that can make plays," SU head coach Jim Boeheim said. "You know, defenses look for him so much that we do give some opportunities to other guys."

Anthony still added the exclamation point, hitting a jumper over Sydmill Harris to push the SU lead to 76-66. On the next possession, he shuffled around Mouton for a two-handed slam, giving Syracuse a 12-point lead, its largest to that point.

Texas made one final push, closing the score to 85-81 with 1:06 left after a Brian Boddicker 3-pointer. But Anthony's layup with 40 seconds remaining

extended the SU advantage to seven, putting the game out of reach.

"So much for the 2-3 zone," Boeheim said. "I knew that it would be an offensive game. Texas can score points against any defense. We haven't really been sharp in the tournament on the offensive end. Tonight, we were right from the beginning."

Syracuse's 55-percent first-half shooting could have finished Texas early. But 20 first-half points from Mouton kept the Longhorns close, and SU led just 48-45 at the break.

Mouton scored the Longhorns' first 10 points and first five field goals. With 9:44 remaining in the first half, Texas trailed, 28-20. At that time, no Longhorn besides Mouton (15 points) and Ford (5) had scored.

SU, meanwhile, touted a balanced first-half attack led by 16 from Anthony. Warrick and McNamara added 10 apiece.

"People forget about our other weapons," SU guard Billy Edelin said. "That works to our advantage."

But Anthony proved to be the biggest advantage.

"He carried us," McNamara said. "Hopefully he can do it again (tonight)." ■

TURNING POINT >>

10:06

After Texas and Syracuse traded baskets for the second half's first 10 minutes, Hakim Warrick's facial over Royal Ivey — posters available soon — capped a 7-1 run from which SU wouldn't look back.

100%

CARMELO-METER

A GAME-BY-GAME INDICATION OF CARMELO ANTHONY'S PERFORMANCE Anthony scored a season-high 33 points on 12-of-19 shooting, grabbed 14 rebounds and had three steals. Anthony saved perhaps his finest game for the biggest stage: the nationally scrutinized, pressure-packed Final Four.

> It doesn't get much better than this. Playing in the national championship game? That's like the biggest event besides the Super Bowl.

CARMELO ANTHONY
SU FORWARD

IN CASE YOU MISSED IT.. A light exploded during the Syracuse press conference yesterday, sending the five starters and SU head coach Jim Boeheim scrambling for cover. When the sparks subsided, Boeheim walked back up on the podium and assessed the situation. He muttered, "Let's get this over with," as he returned to his seat. The press conference continued with the light flaming in the background.

McNamara's presence felt on both ends of the floor

STORY BY PETE IORIZZO

NEW ORLEANS — Another top point guard shut down, but once again, no love for Gerry McNamara.

As T.J. Ford sat despondently in the locker room following the Syracuse men's basketball team's 95-84 win over Texas on Saturday, the Longhorns' star guard was asked about McNamara's defense.

"McNamara?" Ford asked. "What'd he do?"

Turns out he helped negate Ford, holding him to 12 points on 3-of-8 shooting. He also perked the Orangemen's offense, hitting key 3-pointers on his way to a 19-point outing.

Two and a half months ago, after Syracuse beat Seton Hall, 70-66, McNamara scored 17 and held Pirates guard Andre Barrett to 10. Afterward, Barrett questioned McNamara's game and suggested he was a one-dimensional talent.

On Saturday, SU guard Josh Pace challenged that notion.

"He did a good job," Pace said. "He got key steals, and he played within the zone. I'm proud of him."

For good reason, because McNamara's controlled defense threw off the Longhorns' offense. Instead of attacking Ford at the top of the zone, McNamara and SU's other guards played back, enticing Ford to take perimeter shots instead of driving.

As for McNamara's offense, Pace said, "He's been making those tough shots all year long. It's not something that hasn't happened before."

It happened again Saturday, as McNamara sparked Syracuse with his perimeter shooting. Early in the first half, he hit an open 3-pointer that capped an 8-0 run, giving SU a 16-8 advantage. McNamara's second 3 gave the Orangemen a 21-12 lead, their largest of the first half.

"I was hitting my shots early," McNamara said. "That kind of got me going. Once I got my shots early, it kind of carried me through the rest of the game."

Later in the half, McNamara hit a long jumper that looked close to a 3. As the officials checked the replay, chants of "Gerry, Gerry, Gerry" descended from the Louisiana Superdome's upper deck.

The referees ruled that shot a 2-pointer, but McNamara returned to 3-point range later. He hit one with 10:39 left in the game that put Syracuse ahead, 66-61. It came as part of a 15-3 Syracuse run that ran the Longhorns out of the game.

"Every time he puts three points on the board, it's a huge boost for the team," SU center Craig Forth said. "It's like when Hakim (Warrick) dunks. The energy boost is just amazing."

Said McNamara: "That's true because it happened at the right time. A lot of shooters can be that electrifying if they hit their shots at the right time."

Before Saturday, McNamara's shooting had trailed off a bit since earlier in the season. Against Auburn and Oklahoma, he made a combined 2 of 10 3-point tries. Saturday, McNamara nailed 3 of 8 and shot 6 of 12 overall.

"(Ford) turned his back a lot on me when I was off the ball," McNamara said. "I found some open spots, and guys were finding me."

Defensively, McNamara deserves some credit for the Syracuse 2-3 zone's recent tenacity. After recording 10 combined steals in his first five postseason games, McNamara has notched nine in his last two.

Free-throw shooting, for McNamara, has remained consistent. He showed that off Saturday by icing the game with four late free throws. Of course, with Pace and Billy Edelin slam dunking in the last 30 seconds, few noticed.

"I don't worry about that," McNamara said. "If I were a spectator, I wouldn't have noticed me, either." ■

	1	2	F
SYRACUSE	48	47	**95**
TEXAS	45	39	**84**

ORANGEMEN (29-5)	P	R	A
Anthony	33	14	1
McNamara	19	3	4
Warrick	18	7	4
Pace	12	3	2
Edelin	5	3	3
Duany	4	1	0
Forth	2	4	0
McNeil	2	1	0

LONGHORNS (26-7)	P	R	A
Mouton	25	3	3
Buckman	14	7	0
Thomas	13	9	0
Boddicker	12	5	0
Ford	12	4	13
Ivey	4	0	4
Harris	3	0	0
Klotz	1	1	0
Erskin	0	2	0
Ross	0	0	0

Every time he puts three points on the board, it's a huge boost for the team

CRAIG FORTH
ON McNAMARA'S 3-POINTERS

Syracuse beats Kansas in Big Easy for national title

STORY BY PETE IORIZZO | PHOTOS BY AMY YOUNG

NEW ORLEANS — When it finally happened, there were no shouts of jubilation or tears of joy. In fact, Jim Boeheim barely cracked a smile.

Seconds after winning his first national championship — and the first in Syracuse men's basketball history — Boeheim simply walked over to Kansas coach Roy Williams and said congratulations.

"Well, I don't feel any smarter yet," said Boeheim, SU's 27-year head coach. "Maybe tomorrow. As I said before the tournament, I want to win this thing. I'm tremendously happy."

Meanwhile, 15 feet away, the Orangemen danced and celebrated, having just beaten Kansas, 81-78, in front of 54,524 at the Louisiana Superdome. They rejoiced partly out of relief after nearly blowing a 12-point second-half lead.

With 24 seconds left, SU guard Kueth Duany made one of two free throws to give Syracuse an 81-78 lead. Kansas' Kirk Hinrich missed a 3-pointer with 14 seconds left, but the Jayhawks quickly fouled Hakim Warrick, who missed both free throws.

Then Warrick made what will no doubt become the most famous block in Syracuse history. He stretched all 6-foot-8 of his lanky frame to knock away Michael Lee's would-be game-tying 3-point try with 1.5 seconds left.

"I definitely wanted to go out there and just try to make a play after missing the free throws," Warrick said. "I saw a guy open in the corner, and I knew they needed to hit a 3, so I just tried to fly at him. I didn't want it to be another one of those Keith Smart shots."

Kansas had time for one last 3-point try, but Hinrich's desperate heave from the right corner missed everything and safely nestled into Duany's hands.

Minutes after the game, the Syracuse fans chanted "One More Year!" begging Carmelo Anthony, who won the NCAA Tournament's Most Outstanding Player award, to forgo the NBA Draft. Anthony led Syracuse with 20 points and 10 rebounds last night.

"I've never had a feeling like this," Anthony said. "This is the best feeling I've ever had in my life."

After the on-court celebration, Anthony hugged his mother, Mary, who sat in the front row.

"I just told him I love him very much," Mary said as tears streamed down her face. "I'm so proud of him."

Nick Collison and Keith Langford each had 19 points for Kansas. Williams, the Jayhawks' 15-year head coach, now has the second most NCAA Tournament wins of any coach without a national championship.

"This is one of those times I feel so inadequate as a coach and so inadequate as a person," Williams said. "There's nothing I can say to change the way my kids feel, nothing that can change the way I feel."

Despite being down 10 with 6:55 remaining, his Jayhawks never quit. They closed the score to 78-73 after a Hinrich dunk with 2:36 left. SU guard Billy Edelin hit a layup for Syracuse, but Hinrich alley-ooped to Collison to keep the Orangemen's lead at five.

Kansas pulled to within three early in the second half, but poor free-throw shooting held it back in the middle stages. At one point, the Jayhawks missed seven straight from the line.

"You try to make a free throw," Collison said. "You miss, you make,

there's nothing else you can do."

A Bourbon Street-style celebration could have broken out well before midnight on Marshall Street. The Orangemen led, 53-42, at halftime, and their lead ballooned to 18 at one point during the first half behind six 3-pointers and 18 points from Gerry McNamara.

During a 17-5 SU run, McNamara hit back-to-back 3-pointers, putting Syracuse ahead, 23-14, early. McNamara shot 6 of 8 from behind the arc in the first half and 6 of 10 overall.

"I just got off early," McNamara said. "I knew that if we were going to be successful I'd have to make my shots. I got the looks in the first half and the guys carried us in the second half."

The onslaught continued when the Orangemen hit five consecutive shots — including two McNamara 3-pointers — in the half's last seven minutes. After a Duany 3, SU led, 47-29.

Kansas never established its up-tempo game because of Syracuse's first-half 56-percent shooting, including 77 percent from 3-point range. Though the Jayhawks seemed to gain momentum toward halftime, they blew two opportunities to get back in the game.

With Kansas down 12, guard Keith Langford made a dazzling cut from the right corner and hit a layup. That sent the Kansas fans into hysterics, but those feelings quickly subsided when McNamara answered with a 3-pointer.

After Syracuse missed two consecutive shots, Anthony threw a streaking Langford to the ground on his layup try. The referees whistled Anthony for an intentional foul, but Langford missed the second of two free throws.

Then, on the ensuing possession, Hinrich missed a layup, and the Jayhawks lost the ball out of bounds. Anthony drilled a 3-pointer on the other end, giving the Orangemen a 53-40 lead.

After the game, the Orangemen, who pulled out a close one yet again, reflected on the win. Some were lost for words.

"Talk to me in two hours when it hits me," SU center Craig Forth said. "I'll have to sit down. I'm sure every person in the nation will try to describe this. I don't think you can." ∎

SEASON PLAY BY PLAY

THE
DAILY ORANGE

CHAMPIONSHIP EDITION   SYRACUSE'S STUDENT NEWSPAPER **100** CELEBRATING 100 YEARS IN 2003   APRIL 8, 2003 **TUESDAY**

AT LAST

Amy Young / The Daily Orange

Syracuse Orangemen players and coaches pile onto the floor moments after defeating the Kansas Jayhawks in the NCAA men's basketball national championship Monday night in New Orleans.

SU beats Kansas, 81-78, for first basketball national title

BY DARRYL SLATER
ASST. SPORTS EDITOR

After preseason practices, the Syracuse men's basketball team broke huddle with the chant of "Final Four."

Since SU began the season unranked, that notion seemed unlikely.

Now, the Orangemen can call themselves champions.

No. 3-seeded Syracuse won its first NCAA men's basketball championship in school history last night by beating No. 2 Kansas, 81-78, in the Louisiana Superdome. As the clock ticked down, the 11,068 fans who gathered in the Carrier Dome cheered ravenously and bottlenecked out of the arena into steadily falling snow. Fans rushed to Marshall Street, where they danced on the snow-covered sidewalks and

swung from trees. Fireworks crackled above the street, as some fans lit fires and jumped through them.

As the buzzer sounded in New Orleans, SU head coach Jim Boeheim briefly thrust his hands over his head, then walked to center court and calmly shook hands with Kansas head coach Roy Williams. Boeheim's wife, Juli, rushed from the stands and twice planted a kiss on her husband's lips.

In winning his first national title, Boeheim, SU's 27-year head coach, exorcised his ghosts from the '87 championship, also held in the Superdome. In that game, Indiana's Keith Smart hit a shot with four seconds left to snuff SU's hopes.

Before last night, Boeheim had more NCAA Tournament wins (37) than any other active coach who hadn't won a title. Kansas' Williams is now second on that list, with 34 wins.

SU had played in the national title game twice before, losing to Indiana, 74-73, in 1987 and to Kentucky, 76-67, in 1996.

En route to this year's championship, SU beat four Big 12 teams — Oklahoma State, Oklahoma, Texas and Kansas. In doing so, Syracuse experience to win a national title. All season, the Orangemen started
SEE **RECAP** PAGE 8

3 **M-STREET MADNESS** Students take to the streets, burning T-shirts and whooping it up

4 **PACKED HOUSE** More than 11,000 fans cheer on Syracuse in the Carrier Dome

20 **MELO DRAMA** Anthony scores 20 points, earning Most Valuable Player honors

Orangemen rode season's waves together all year

COLUMN BY PETE IORIZZO

NEW ORLEANS — Rumors circulated this weekend that soon after the Syracuse men's basketball team's charter flight to the Big Easy took off last Wednesday, a few Orangemen felt a little queasy. And this was more than a case of pre-Final Four butterflies.

Supposedly, the plane took a 10-second nosedive, sending players, coaches and administrative assistants into hysterics.

The story turned out to be false, but hey, would it have been so surprising if it were true? This entire season has, after all, been a wild ride, culminating last night in an on-court celebration and net-cutting ceremony, as the Orangemen beat Kansas, 81-78, to win the first national championship in school history.

The Orangemen's mere appearance in the national championship game was a vindication, an honor for a group of 15 players that brought this university, this city, on a roller coaster ride so fun even Jim Boeheim has been smiling. Well, smirking, at least.

Today, the Orangemen, and the rest of us, can step off the ride onto the platform and take a deep breath. There's no reason to be sorry the ride's over. Just celebrate because it happened.

Consider that, one year ago, Syracuse played in the NIT Final Four. In between arrests and in-fighting, that group learned to lose basketball games. Heck, they practically earned a Ph.D. in it. Roller coaster ride? More like train wreck.

But this year's Orangemen have been different from the start. Six months ago, before Carmelo was King and Gerry was Golden and Billy was back, they came together as a group after each practice, put their hands together and shouted, in unison, "Final Four!"

"That's what we'd say after every practice," SU guard Josh Pace said softly, reflecting on those practices that seem so long ago. "We really believed we could get here."

We laughed at them then. Final Four? Come on. Not one year removed from a car-accident season, and certainly not with four underclassmen starters, including two freshmen.

Then Syracuse dropped the season opener to Memphis at Madison Square Garden. The Orangemen missed foul shots down the stretch and played like freshmen. Who knew it'd be the last time that would happen?

"Phew, I don't even remember that to tell you the truth," SU center Craig Forth said. "I probably didn't score though," he added laughing, something he's done more of this season.

"We played well," Boeheim said of the Memphis game. "We played well during the middle of the year. We played well at the end of the year. We've been playing well in the tournament."

So when, then, did the whole city hop on board? When did the rest of us start believing what the Orangemen believed all along?

Maybe somewhere in the midst of three court rushings after a home win against Pittsburgh. Or perhaps when Syracuse won three tough road games — at Michigan State, Notre Dame and Georgetown. Or it could've happened when Carmelo Anthony extended an invitation in the form of a Final Four guarantee.

Admittedly, just like after those early season Final Four chants, we chuckled at Anthony's audacity. And we're still smiling now, because, regardless of last night, the Orangemen have given this community so much to celebrate.

Before Sunday's practice, the last of the season, the Orangemen used their latest rallying cry.

"Together!" their collective voices echoed through the cavernous, empty Superdome.

"Together," Pace said. "That's what we say now. We win together, we lose together."

Last night, they won together. And this season, they brought this city together. ∎

SEASON PLAY BY PLAY

Travels with Andrew: A journey to the Final Four

STORY BY DANIEL RIVERO

It's a bit uncomfortable, disturbing even, to imagine Student Association President Andrew Thomson as your typical college student.

He is, after all, more like your cocky professor than he is your roommate — a decision-maker in student affairs and a crowned king in bureaucratic chess. Sometimes you just have to wonder: hidden somewhere amongst his swamp of suits and ties, his presidential uniform, does the guy own any jeans?

Thomson shook off his SA persona Thursday afternoon and became cool, casual and ... college. He did something more anarchist than parliamentarian. Thomson abandoned classes and meetings to join the legions of Syracuse University fans who took off on a road trip to the Big Easy late last week to cheer for the Orangemen in the Final Four.

He crammed his burgundy Plymouth Neon with cameras, magazines, music and his childhood friend.

"How's it going Andrew? Want me to read you some Playboy?" asked Jesse Desper, a sophomore political science major at Hobart College.

"The pictures or the articles?" said Thomson in his naturally deadpan voice.

"Whatever you want," said Desper, with a sly smile.

Desper, whose relationship with Thomson is more kid brother than average friend, served as the Technicolor entertainment to a 20-hour drive through gray roads, parades of battlefield memorial signs and the unintentionally creepy South.

He manages four hours into the trip to blow the cigarette lighter fuse that powers the portable CD player — a fuse for which Thomson later stops at a Wal-Mart to buy — rolls down his window to ask strangers if they want to join them in the ride to New Orleans and challenges Thomson to a game of "Name that Tune."

"That's another point for me, bitch," Thomson said, after he finally scored by identifying the punky serenade of Sum-41's "Still Waiting." It's no use, however. He never quite catches up to Desper's 10-point lead. To be fair, Thomson did drive the entire trip.

At about 2 a.m. Friday, the boys rolled into Virginia Tech, a school that oozed imagination by naming its buildings with colorful catch phrases, like New Residence Hall East.

Thomson and Desper spent the night in the dorm of Scott Edmond, a third-year architecture student and another of Thomson's Maine buddies who would join him on the trip. Desper took the top bunk, with Thomson on the futon.

It was at Virginia Tech where Thomson and Desper learned a bit more about the stranger they were staying with in New Orleans. A friend of a friend of Edmond's, they were told she was a 34-year-old potential stripper, whose boyfriend had once smoked three bowls of marijuana to alleviate his anxiety in meeting strangers.

"Eh, it's college," Thomson said. "I've seen worse."

After a bite to eat in one of the university's food courts Friday (no SUpercard accepted), it was back on the road for the crew with many more state lines to cross.

"Tennessee looks like a giant golf course," Thomson said of the rolling cow pastures.

It was not until the car got to Alabama that the road trippers became mildly amused by the distinct difference from the Northeast. Cell phones changed time zones automatically, the climate became warmer and Desper analyzed Southern hospitality.

"These Southern folks talk really strange," he said after a cereal stop at Food World grocery store. "I mean, I'm lazy, too. But come on."

Thomson, who had hoped to escape from the SA world, received various telephone calls as the boys got closer to their destination. They were all from Assembly members, some of who had a little too much to drink and were ratting out other members for not showing up to meetings ("Like if I could do anything," Thomson said). Or just asking him to have Gerry McNamara call them from Bourbon Street.

Finally, after stops at many a sketchy gas station and eating too much fast food, the boys reached New Orleans but had little luck getting directions to just about anywhere.

"Baby, I don't even know where I am," an over-partied 20-something blonde woman said to Desper as the car passed in front of Harrah's Casino.

Moments later, Thomson dropped off the embedded reporter at the Hyatt and left to where he would be staying at for the duration of their trip — the home of a New Orleans strip-club worker for what could arguably be one of the wildest times of his non-jean-wearing college years. ■

Team adds extra reason to party in New Orleans

STORY BY DANIEL RIVERO AND JUSTIN YOUNG

NEW ORLEANS — They were tears that sparkled orange.

Rodney Williams doesn't cry, but seeing the Orangemen defeat the Jayhawks on Monday night, he had to give in.

Williams, a Syracuse fan since 1983, said he only initially saw this year's team going to the Sweet 16.

"Carmelo makes it look so effortless," Williams said. "I cannot believe it, I'm just so happy."

Happy? An understatement.

Moments after SU's first-ever NCAA championship, Williams was just one of the ecstatic fans who took control of the surrounding areas of the Louisiana Superdome and Bourbon Street, sucking and evaporating any and all air of bitterness brought forth by the seemingly displeased Kansas fans. Piggy back rides, sitting on shoulders, gorilla-strength hugs, unstoppable "We're No. 1" cheers, beer and strings of "Let's go Orange" chants — it was all mayhem and it was all over New Orleans.

And to think, Williams almost left Saturday for Houston.

"My uncle, my cousin, they are all Texas fans and wanted to leave Saturday, but I told them, 'You can't do that to me,'" Williams said.

It is no surprise either that many of the Syracuse basketball team's student fans, many of whom have already put classes on hold to attend the Final Four, are having second thoughts about when to make their way back to the frigid north. Most fans heading to Bourbon Street after the win promised to celebrate till their bodies allowed it.

"This is the happiest moment of my college career," said Dan Kalagvano, a sophomore finance major.

Kalagvano, on his way to Bourbon, said he planned to head back to campus Tuesday morning, depending of course on his condition after the parties. Robert Becker, who also planned to celebrate at Bourbon for the night, said Monday's win was also a definitive moment in his college experience.

"This is the greatest moment as a fan," said Becker, a sophomore management major. "I don't think you have to be a player to understand how good this feels."

Chris Macewan, a 1999 SU finance grad, who flew from Rochester to Pensacola, Fla., and drove from Pensacola to New Orleans, said he didn't anticipate the win but would be ready for Monday night. Other SU fans were a bit less eloquent in their reaction.

"It's New Orleans, so fuck school," said Collin Barletta, an undecided sophomore who flew from New York City.

Barletta is planning on flying back Wednesday but is not going to let his missed classes interfere with his celebration, which will last into early Tuesday in the French Quarter. He even started early, clutching a Heineken during the SU pep rally in the late afternoon.

His friend Lou Giangrande, a sophomore television, radio and film major, won't enjoy the option of having soft drinks and peanuts to soothe a hangover. Giangrande drove down to Louisiana and is going to have to face the open road if he hopes to get back to the Hill before his test at 10:40 a.m. Wednesday. Even his compatriots doubt an on-time arrival, but he may have an even bigger problem, namely what his Anthropology 111 test is on.

"I am going to find out when I study on the way back," he said.

Rob Froliech found one sure-fire way to enjoy the nightlife worry-free. The Orangeman fan took a flight down after work at Darwin's on Saturday.

"Forget Cuse'n it up," said Froliech, a dropout of SU. "I am stayin'." ■

Students weigh benefits, expense of following team

STORY BY JUSTIN YOUNG | CONTRIBUTING WRITER JOHN NUTHALL

NEW ORLEANS — Beyond the last-minute heroics and the untold promise of a national championship lies a reality for Syracuse basketball fans as harsh as a Jeremy McNeil shot-block.

As the Orangemen marched from Boston to Albany and now on to New Orleans, their fans followed. Some packed tight into cars and even tighter into hotel rooms just to see Carmelo and company eliminate all comers. Although they undoubtedly gained memories not soon forgotten, the monetary price paid will probably not elicit the same fond memories.

This fact is especially true for those who plan to migrate to the Big Easy to witness SU tangle with Texas on Saturday in the Louisiana Superdome. The cross-country trip is not a cheap one. Between travel, lodging, food and the tickets themselves, a member of the Orange faithful is looking at a hefty bill with no guarantee that his team will even be in contention after Saturday.

To break down the cost you have to start at the beginning — tickets. Hundreds huddled in front of Carrier Dome Gate E in the snowy weather to garner seats ranging from $120 to $180. But tickets did not sell out until 15 minutes before the box offices were set to close-up shop at 4 p.m, said Carrier Dome General Manager Pat Campbell. Those who did not make it down to the Dome might have to try their luck on Internet auction site eBay, where a trio of tickets and a Carmelo

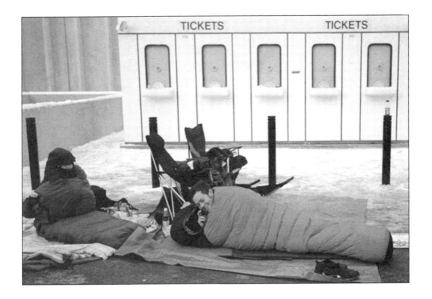

Anthony autographed edition of this very paper has not yet met it's opening bid of $1,1999.99.

The trip down South will prove far less cost-efficient for residents of the Hill than did the East Regional finals in Albany, a measly two-hour jaunt compared to the 20-hour journey to New Orleans. T.J. Basalla and five of his friends all made the trip to see the Albany games, utilizing an early '90s Pontiac. Basalla, a freshman broadcast journalism major, said he dropped about $250 in total for his weekend, a far cry from Cheaptickets.com's flight listings that do not drop below $1,668 for a weekend round trip or the 1,396 mile drive with gas prices hovering around $1.50 to $1.70 per gallon.

Hotel accommodations might prove to be an equally daunting task. A fan would be hard pressed to find a room for less than $150 per night, with many requiring a minimum of nights that guests must stay. The Hampton Inn, which will receive four bus-loads of Syracuse fans Friday, encouraged using one room to house many guests.

"(Our suite) sleeps a lot of people," said Fred Pepper, assistant manager. "You can just pile 'em on in."

Pepper's suite will run one lucky group of collegiate basketball enthusiasts $249 a night with a minimum of 4 nights. He added that the current price is upped from what the hotel normally charges when there is not an event of this magnitude in town.

After making it to the bayou and plunking down your guaranteed $996 (plus tax) for a place to stay, room service might be the last thing on your mind. The New Orleans Shopping Centre at the Dome provides a cheaper mall food court alternative for those looking to cut corners. A sample of the fine cuisine includes La Rue's Gourmet To Go, The Steak Escape, Subway and even Kimmel-throwback Sbarros, where homesick Orangemen can munch on a slice of stuffed spinach and pepperoni pizza for $4.

Basalla said he never entertained notions of coming to Louisiana, largely because of scheduling conflicts but also his own fiscal restraints.

"I am just a college student," he said. "I don't have that much money." ■

New Orleans fans default to bars for spectating

STORY BY DANIEL RIVERO AND JUSTIN YOUNG

NEW ORLEANS — People don't get drunk in New Orleans. They get smashed.

Instead of breathing oxygen, conquered noses and lungs operate by the air of liquor, eardrums begin to play the bongo and smoking a cigar is as cool as casual sex.

Not surprisingly, the next best spot to catch the Final Four games if you didn't get tickets to the Superdome was a local bar. Both the Hyttops Sports Bar at the Hyatt and the lobby-turned-bar at the Marriott filled to capacity Saturday night as the Orangemen played Texas in the semifinals of the college basketball championship.

Hyttops, the closest bar to the Superdome, was infested with mourning Marquette fans, who were joined by members of the team themselves during the first half, drinking away memories of their lopsided loss to Kansas. Clearly, they were not cheering for Syracuse.

The bar, with Budweiser stands scattered throughout the lounge area, was equipped with two 10-foot-tall television screens and enough beer to rile the crowd.

"You suck Carmelo. Go back to 'Cuse," a Texas fan said loudly during the action.

The Marriott, where the Syracuse team called home, was unmistakably Orange territory this weekend, with only a brief lull during the game itself when Longhorn fans staged a momentary coup de tat.

Joe Ovalle, a San Francisco resident who was at the Marriott on

Saturday, said he supported the Orangemen because his eighth-grade teacher Ms. Jarvac was from Syracuse.

As the Orangemen fans received some friendly banter from Texas fans, Keith Wade, along with his wife Maria, from Ann Arbor, Mich., became a little excited.

"I was going to be calm until they started talking, actin' a fool," he said.

Wade, whose daughter Briana is a freshman track runner at SU, said the bar was the best seat in the house. He predicted that the end of the Syracuse-Texas game would have the Orangemen on top 76-71 but still hinged his plans for the rest of the evening on the outcome.

"If we win, we are hitting Bourbon," he said. "If we lose, we are hitting Decatur Street and sitting in the dark."

Wade, who has gone to see every Final Four since 1990, couldn't get four tickets together by Saturday. But he still saw members of the team Thursday night on Bourbon Street. All fans, though, had the opportunity to see the players earlier in the day, when the Orange-dominated Marriott hosted the team pep rally.

Chants of "Let's go Orange" diffused throughout the Preservation Hall Ballroom as the cheerleaders, Otto the Orange, the Dance Team, the Sour Sitrus Society and an ever-present supply of beer pumped the fans up for the game. Sean McDonough, an SU graduate and announcer for the Boston Red Sox, was the master of ceremonies for the rally and became the collective voice for the fans.

"We let the people in New Orleans know the 'Cuse is in the house," he said.

Chancellor Kenneth A. Shaw, who was in the house as much as he was out of Syracuse, entertained the fans with a quick story. He spoke of how he talked to Board of Trustees Chairman Joe Lampe, who said he couldn't go to the game because he was redoing his bathroom. Shaw, surprisingly, saw him in New Orleans. How did he make it?

"He said, 'We have been used to an outdoor John this long. We can continue,' " Shaw said.

Other attendees included Syracuse Mayor Matt Driscoll, who called the Orangemen the best team in the United States, and assistant coach Bernie Fine.

"We came down in '87 and we feel we have some unfinished business," said Fine, referring to the narrow loss to Indiana. He said that if SU won the championship, "the chancellor is in room 4612 and said the drinks are on him."

As Saturday's game came to an end, Syracuse fans in the Big Easy prepared to party and look ahead.

"This was one of the best games they've played, but they're clicking. They seem to be open to Monday," said John Osbourne, team manager in 1992. "Everyone loves this team."

"I feel they're gonna win it all. Carmelo is unstoppable," said Steve Fassinger, whose dad graduated from SU decades ago and who has been a fan since he was 8 years old. "I went to see the Final Four in '96, and they didn't win it, but this, I'm thrilled."

SU seniors Andrea Goldman, a speech communication major, and Yara Koht, a retail major, said they now looked forward to getting a ticket for Monday's game.

The two students decided to head down to New Orleans on Thursday, arrived Friday and met somebody in the Garden District Hotel, where they were staying, who sold them two tickets at $100 apiece.

"We know they are going to win," Koht said. ∎

For homey feel, students gather in dorms for game

STORY BY JOHN NUTHALL

While most Syracuse University students packed into the Dome to watch the Orangemen claim the national title, handfuls of students clustered around televisions to enjoy the game with a few close friends rather than thousands of screaming fans.

One group of eight friends gathered on the ground floor lounge of Brewster/Boland to watch. Over a smorgasbord of cookies, chips and pizza from Domino's, they waved frantically at the TV every time Kansas forward Nick Collison stepped to the free-throw line, erupted with every Kueth Duany 3-pointer and offered a running critique of forward Craig Forth's performance. But it took some of the group until halftime to realize the true importance of the occasion.

"Hey, I just realized that we're in the championship," said Marquith Muhammad, a freshman industrial design major. "It just doesn't seem real to me."

When the obligatory halftime war report interrupted a Swedish Fish food fight, the eight refused to let it dampen their spirits.

"What they don't really know is that Saddam is in the U.S. watching the game, and he's rooting for Kansas," joked Claudedian Cerat, a freshman political science major.

The friends were well aware that few students were enjoying the game the same way they were. For them, the reason for skipping the Dome party was a mixture of economics and atmosphere. Muhammad said that he wanted to to be able to talk to his friends during the game.

THE FINAL FOUR

"Plus, its cheap, which is always a good reason when you're in college," Muhammad added.

Though the all-freshman group has been together since they met during the university's SummerStart program, they started watching basketball together during the last few weeks of the tournament. They met in the same spot and in the exact same seats to watch SU vanquish Texas on Saturday night.

In the second half, the group was tight-lipped and nervous, alternately silencing nay-sayers and knocking on the Formica table to avoid jinxing a Syracuse victory. When Muhammad warned that Kansas' Kirk Hinrich might catch fire, a hail of tortilla chips forced him to defend his position.

"I'm just saying the facts," Muhammad said. "You can't get mad at the facts."

When the Orangemen were only a 3-pointer away from losing it all in the game's final minutes, all eight friends were on their feet and silent. As the final seconds ran down, the scene changed. The group ran a lap around the Brewster/Boland lobby before charging out into the snow to join the mob of fans on Marshall Street. ■

Thousands flock to M-Street for second night of havoc

STORY BY RYAN GAINOR | CONTRIBUTING WRITERS DARRYL SLATER AND SEAN MILLS

Maybe it was the ounces upon ounces of alcohol consumed during the game. Or, perhaps, the beginnings of an April snowstorm. Likely, it was simply winning a national title.

Thousands of Syracuse University students flocked from dorms, the Carrier Dome and bars to celebrate on Marshall Street. And celebrate they did. More than 100 police greeted the fans, barricaded crowds, put out fires and, generally, tried to subdue the mass.

The crowd, significantly larger than Saturday's, filled Marshall Street, spilling onto the outlying South Crouse and University avenues. Students climbed trees, greased earlier in the day to protect against such actions, and turned them into kindling. They rocked them until they fell, added their shirts and sparked away, better lighting the vision for women, and men, flashing the crowd.

"Within five minutes, we saw a guy naked in a tree, a homeless guy, a guy in a chicken suit and a bonfire," said Lindsay Skorupa, a sophomore English and textual studies major.

Several times, officers escorted fire officials to those blazes. At one point, officials put out a fire, in front of Jay's Communications, that stretched about 8 feet into the air.

"The cops did a great job, they didn't break up the fires as fast as they did last time and just let everyone have a good time," said freshman architecture major Mark Wizeman.

THE FINAL FOUR

Accompanying the larger crowd were more than 100 Syracuse police officers in riot gear, more than doubling the number present after SU's win over Texas, Lt. John Brennan said. Many of those officers guarded business behind a line of wooden dollys, diverting pedestrians into the closed-off street. Other officers perched themselves atop M-Street businesses to look over the crowd.

"As long as students keep orderly and there is no criminal mischief, students can stay in the streets," Brennan said.

For officers, criminal mischief was in the cards. Several students used a metal pipe to break apart a parking meter, others destroyed trees and set fires. Syracuse Police spokesman Sgt. Tom Connellan could not comment on the number but said arrests had been made.

"It is mostly going well," he said. "But it will be a long night."

The officers' nights included being pelted with snow balls and having glass bottles thrown at them.

One of the people taken into police custody and charged with second degree harassment was SU graduate Justin Silverman. Silverman,

publisher of the greek newspaper Hermes, was on Marshall Street taking photos behind the police dollys when an officer confronted him about his press credentials, he said. Silverman showed the officer a New York State Press Association pass and was allowed to stay. Minutes later, another officer confronted him and tried removing Silverman from the sidewalk. Silverman resisted, at which point the officer told him press access does not give him permission to do whatever he wants and handcuffed him in the street. Silverman will contest the misdemeanor in court.

While Silverman waited for some time on the street, officers had others wait in a bright yellow school bus. There, they had ample opportunity to discuss the reasons for their arrests. And maybe a bit about the game.

Many on Marshall Street had just those discussions. They still could

not believe SU won a national championship. The ghosts of Keith Smart's last-second shot to defeat the Orangemen in the 1987 championship game seemed forgotten, replaced with the all-too vital image of Carmelo Anthony and his teammates.

Jason Roche, a 1994 graduate, no longer needs to harbor those faded images. And he came back to M-Street to help make that happen.

"I have been waiting for this for as long as I can remember," he said.

As officers began dispersing the crowd at about 1 a.m., some wanted their pyrotechnics and partying to go on. And so the party, for some with lighters, traveled the short distance to Walnut Place. An unidentified person set fire to a couch across the street from the Alpha Tau Omega fraternity house. Students threw snow balls as firefighters put out the blaze.

But setting fires was just another sign of support for the team, said Tony Namdar, a sophomore management major.

"It was symbolic for the school cause the fire was orange," he said. ∎

THE FINAL FOUR

Photography Credits

Front & back cover photos by Natalia Jimenez

9 Zack Seckler

14 Natalia Jimenez

20 Amy Young

22 Amy Young

24 Amy Young

28 James Pinsky

31 Seth Siditsky

36 Natalia Jimenez

39 Amy Young

43 Amy Young

49 Amy Young

51 Amy Young

54 James Pinsky

59 James Pinsky

63 Amy Young

68 Natalia Jimenez

290 Amy Young

292 Seth Siditsky

295 Natalia Jimenez

296 Natalia Jimenez

298 Amy Young

302 Jenny Dean

304 Amy Young

305 Jenny Dean

306 Seth Siditsky

307 Natalia Jimenez

308 Jenny Dean

309 Natalia Jimenez

310 Natalia Jimenez

Acknowledgements

The Daily Orange would like to thank the editors, writers, photographers and friends who made this book possible:

Katie Bartholomew

Nicole Begin

Ben Bloker

Tito Bottitta

Chris Carlson

Phil Carlucci

Andrea Cowsert

Colin Dabkowski

Jenny Dean

Ryan Gainor

Ashleigh Graf

Chico Harlan

Pete Iorizzo

Natalia Jimenez

Eric Jukelevics

Adam Kilgore

Scott Lieber

David Merriell

Pete Moore

John Nuthall

Monica Padluck

Joe Paymond

James Pinsky

Daniel Rivero

Eli Saslow

Pete Schreiber

Zack Seckler

Seth Siditsky

Tracy Simpson

Darryl Slater

Peter Waack

Amy Young

Justin Young